SMITTEN

THE WAY
of the
BRILLIANT FLIRT

ARIEL KILEY & SIMONE KORNFELD

CHRONICLE BOOKS
SAN FRANCISCO

Library of Congress Cataloging-in-Publication Data:

Kiley, Ariel.
  Smitten : the way of the brilliant flirt / by Ariel Kiley and Simone Kornfeld.
    p. cm.
  ISBN 978-1-4521-1675-4
  1. Flirting. 2. Man-woman relationships. 3. Dating (Social customs) I.
Kornfeld, Simone. II. Title.

  HQ801.K52 2013
  306.73—dc23

2012034123

Manufactured in China

Designed by Hillary Caudle
Cover design by Jennifer Tolo Pierce
Composited by Cody Gates, Happenstance Type-O-Rama

10 9 8 7 6 5 4 3 2 1

Chronicle Books LLC
680 Second Street
San Francisco, California 94107
www.chroniclebooks.com

FOR MARLENA, GRACE, AND BIANCA

ACKNOWLEDGMENTS

We are deeply grateful to the following people for their support in the creation and publication of *Smitten*.

To Brianne Johnson and Michelle Rubin of Writers House. To Lisa Tauber, Lorena Jones, Claire Fletcher, Doug Ogan, Jennifer Tolo Pierce, Debra DeFord-Minerva, and Leigh Haber of Chronicle Books. To William Clark, Alex Griessmann, Paige Smith, Will Stewart, and Dylan Gary. To our fathers: Poppy, Dudley, and Steve. To our grandmothers: Annie, Alice, Nona Bianca, and Patricia. To the colorful array of men we've had the great pleasure of flirting with over the years. And to the coven: Ride or die, witches.

CONTENTS

INTRODUCTION

PART ONE:
UNVEILING YOUR LUMINESCENCE
Laying the Groundwork for Masterful Flirtation

PART TWO:
THE WAY OF THE BRILLIANT FLIRT
The 8 Earth-Shattering Flirtation Techniques

CONCLUSION

INTRODUCTION

———◈◈◈———

Flirting, as a concept, doesn't always get the credit it deserves. It tends to bring to mind Betty Boop's furiously fluttering eyelashes and submissive squeaks or the cunning captain of the cheerleading squad who mysteriously brainwashed the guy you were going steady with all summer. We often think of flirtation as a cheap trick used to satisfy feeble self-esteem and wicked intentions. These misconceptions, unfortunately, tend to make us tentative and ineffective flirts, which spoils our potential to attract the men we desire. But becoming an amazing flirt is not about using tawdry tricks and sly traps to get what we want, nor is it about having abnormally plump lips or the ripest rear in the room. Being a great flirt is a natural byproduct of being a confident, engaged, unique woman who can't help but let her true self shine, causing the whole world to become enraptured by her unencumbered spirit.

Many of us have never really mastered effective flirtation, so we often find ourselves chickening out before even giving it a shot. Which might look something like this: You're at a midsummer bluegrass fest waiting in line for the Porta-Potty when the scruffy guy behind you flashes an inviting smile. You are immediately drawn to his country charm, but you're also flooded with uncertainty about how to respond, which causes you to dart into the stall, lock the door, and then exit sheepishly, avoiding his eyes on the way out. Then you waste the rest of the night mourning the missed opportunity. On the other hand, sometimes we are so overwhelmed by the pressure that we unwittingly sabotage our chances, which might look like this: You are out with your girlfriends at the new Italian trattoria and you've been making eyes at the dangerously handsome owner all evening. Toward the end of the meal, he makes his way over and asks if you'd like to try a taste of his special reserve grappa. You happily accept, but when he pulls up a chair, you're suddenly so tongue-tied that you only manage to utter a few lame niceties, and the conversation dwindles into awkward silence. Before you know it he's corked up his grappa and risen from the table, and you're left kicking yourself for having ruined your Romanesque romance forever.

Even if we make it past those first few rocky moments and find ourselves in conversation with an attractive gentleman, our attempts at flirtation are often lame. This is because we repress our true impulses, squelch our honest expression, and don't allow our inner light to shine—which happens every time we refrain from busting out the lyrics to our favorite pop song for fear he'll think we're too weird. Or every time we are so preoccupied with how our skin looks in the light or how our dress fits over our hips that we don't allow ourselves the freedom to actually be present during the interaction. It happens every time we restrict ourselves to the typical conversation topics for fear he'll be turned off if we discuss the details of our latest summer solstice séance. Basically, it's every time we shrink into an agreeable ball of mush for fear our honest self will scare him off.

In the world of *Smitten,* brilliant flirtation is an art—the art of openly expressing our truest selves and causing a man to fall head over heels with us at first flirt. By learning the *Smitten* way, you will gain the confidence to let your own unique inner light shine so you are able to render any man thoroughly enthralled during the first encounter or first date. You heard us right—there is no need to cut off your kookiness or plug up your squeaky singing voice. No need to look like a svelte Eastern European giantess or only be seen under the flattering glow of low-wattage bulbs. You are going to learn how to be *so free* during the first encounter or first date with an appealing gentleman that you will not even consider the possibility that you could say the wrong thing or somehow not measure up—let alone fall prey to the desperation and anxiety that are the hallmarks of flirtation disasters.

Undeniable and indestructible, your sparkling inner light is your strongest asset in the game of love. However, most of us are not acquainted with this inner light or don't quite trust in its appeal. The journey through *Smitten* will move you into a process of self-realization so you can gain confidence in who you truly are and finally take hold of this most powerful asset. Your emblazoned authenticity is the force that will allow any variation of male to become wholly beguiled with your exquisitely true, wildly rapturous self.

Smitten is not the ordinary *Play the Game Right and Prince Charming Will Come Save You* kind of book. It is a book for ladies who'd rather not settle for a life stifled by mediocrity and dysfunction. You will not be asked to compromise yourself or manipulate men. There will be no lessons on arbitrarily canceling dates, hanging up the phone before he does, or demanding a marriage proposal after a year of dating. Those rules of attraction are petty, contrived, inauthentic, and downright mean. Frankly, it doesn't turn us on to approach a relationship as if it were a combat zone. In the *Smitten* philosophy, brilliant flirtation is about baring your true essence, rather than sharing frilly fabrications. It's expressing your genuine self instead of engaging in invented ideals. It's having the awareness, courage, and confidence to stay rooted in your authenticity under any romantic circumstance.

In order for you to become the blissfully enlightened man magnet you were born to be, the journey through *Smitten* is divided into two distinct parts. Part One: Unveiling Your Luminescence is designed to help you get in touch with your sizzling inner light by jump-starting your process of self-realization. With your luminescence on high, you will be fully prepared to take on Part Two: The Way of the Brilliant Flirt. In this section, we present the eight flirtation techniques that will tap into your authenticity and allow you to attract all the men you could ever desire.

We make no judgements about how you utilize the fruitful information that lies ahead. Whether you're seeking two tickets to paradise with your soul mate or just want the skills to inspire a few broiling minutes of desire with a stranger, we're not here to judge. We aren't out to promote the pursuit of marriage when you are actually just out to enjoy the art of attraction, nor do we advocate denying your longing for a life partner for a mere "seven minutes in heaven." Friendly flirtation can be used to simply brighten the day; a few playful moments with the concessions guy scooping your popcorn could really butter up the afternoon. Or it can be used to lay the groundwork for a lifelong relationship with your future husband.

Furthermore, though we discuss heterosexual interactions throughout the book, these teachings are relevant for all sorts of romantic relationships. Whether you're gay, lesbian, straight, bi, transgender, transsexual, not yet sure, or would rather not define, the pearls of *Smitten*'s wisdom can be used to enhance your self-knowledge and flirting skills in any arena. Lastly, we are women writing from a woman's perspective, but that doesn't mean guys can't benefit from the wellspring of astuteness and acumen documented in these pages. We encourage you men to learn all you can from our teachings. We want to see your sizzling inner light too!

Given the fact that we do not possess doctorates, master's degrees, or even bachelor's degrees on the topic of self-realization, and we have yet to find a school that offers a minor in flirtation, it seems appropriate for us to give you a glimpse into our personal histories to illuminate our top-notch credentials in both of these subjects. We've had to work hard to acquire our knowledge and apply every inch of ourselves to our studies. You see, our flirtation skills weren't always so exquisitely honed; we weren't always able to enrapture the opposite sex with such effortless grace. Years ago, we were mere novices in the art of brilliant flirtation.

OUR JOURNEY TO FLIRTATION MASTERY

We met on the first day of the first week of our theater training at New York University. After having been instructed by a professor to "freely interpret our inner animal," we exchanged our first stealthy glance of skepticism. Nevertheless, we soon found ourselves crawling around on the floor amidst our fellow befuddled freshmen. And although most of our classmates that semester were quickly preoccupied with dorm-room drama and dining hall dinner menus, both of us knew we had bigger fish to fry. It wasn't long before we discovered our mutual desire; we each craved an all-access key to the greatest city on Earth (where else can you get sweet-potato pierogies and a chocolate shake at 4 A.M. on a Sunday?).

Our shared ambition propelled us to search out the most adventurous evenings, to mix with the most interesting individuals, and to indulge our most insatiable appetites for all things extraordinary. We were in pursuit of a dream of urban opulence.

The summer of 2001 was the culmination of our first two years of friendship. Free of the limiting schedule of academia, we frolicked unencumbered throughout the steamy streets of Manhattan. Equipped with barely passable fake IDs, we grabbed every opportunity to get into the newest nightclubs, and eagerly met and mingled with whomever we encountered—from fashionistas to Wall Street types to the latest flash-in-the-pan celebrities. Our nights soon became a haze of lavish cocktails, leather pants, smoky eyes, and sultry looks.

There's nothing quite like the intoxicating high of finally being *seen*—noticed and admired in a grown-up world of glitz and glamour. But such ego gratification is fleeting; it is a persistent hunger that must be constantly fed. Caught in the dizzying spiral of the nightlife high, we were forever searching for our next fix. Then, as it happens when young attention junkies are on the prowl for admiration, those dreamy midsummer nights soon spawned male entanglements. We both found ourselves with boyfriends.

Simone's pick was a waify aspiring model who could get her into nearly any nightclub with just a slight tip of his low baseball cap. There were just a few minor issues, such as his still living at home with his mother, his lying about being 23 when he was actually 28, and, of course, his stealing Simone's Nars Black Moon eyeliner to fill in his not-well-defined mole. (Why couldn't he have taken her cheap drug store backup?) Then there was that one unfortunate night when she fell asleep with bloody toes after he'd dragged her across the street in a fit of wanton jealousy. But all was soon well; the waif redeemed himself by buying her an expensive birthday gift—with only one teeny catch: He'd purchased it by snatching her ATM card and pilfering money from her bank account. How very thoughtful of him.

Meanwhile, Ariel was lucky enough to begin a relationship with a dashing young writer she fell for while serving him Pabst at a West Village dive. At the time, this blue-eyed charmer was both homeless and jobless, but that didn't bother him. He simply crashed at Ariel's place, ate her food, soiled her sheets, and used up all the quarters for the laundry machine. He would often disappear for days at a time, returning only when he longed for the comfort of a warm bed and the breast once more. It wasn't too much later when she learned that in actuality, he had a sizeable trust fund that helped support his covert cocaine habit, was sleeping with one of her co-waitresses, and, worst of all, his precious writer's pad (the contents of which he implied would one-up Updike himself) turned out to be blank. But young Ariel still couldn't resist her roaming writer, even after his eerie exegesis on wanting to join the army so he could kill a man without legal consequence.

Even the phoniest of soothsayers could foresee disaster written all over our boyfriend selections. It's not that we were dense; we just weren't that interested in reading the tea leaves. It wasn't yet part of our operating systems to question why we were attracted to these men and the real significance behind our decisions to be with them. Even if we were peripherally aware that such self-inquiry could improve our situations, we weren't quite ready to give it a go. But by the end of that summer, those wild nights ended and the relationships crashed and burned. We had little to show for all that "fun" besides confusion, anger, disappointment, and really, really puffy eyes.

Then the World Trade Center towers came down.

As tragedy overtook the city, our lives, like those of so many others, were forced into perspective. With gray-white ash drifting through our windows and the smell of burning chemicals filling the Village's streets, we could hardly recognize our previous selves. Alarmed by our past brazen behavior, we both receded into ourselves. From within, we looked for something to hold on to, a hint of clarity that might assist us in finding more stable ground.

Post-college found us in two different cities with two very different lives. In Burlington, Vermont, Ariel was living in solitude, consumed with a raw food diet and her mission to master the guitar. In Los Angeles, Simone had taken up residence with a new puppy and was focused on housebreaking and the efficacy of essential oils in carpet stain removal. Our circumstances differed, yet our new goals were similar. We had shifted from looking outward for power and gratification to looking inward for meaning and balance. Instead of gorging on forest mushroom pâté and French martinis, our evenings were spent digesting the densest material on self-discovery that we could find. Long-distance phone conversations were centered on our latest spirituality and psychology reads. We focused on integrating the mind, body, and spirit, and actually became interested in expressing that "inner animal" we had scoffed at years before.

Though our studies during this time were quite valuable to our personal development, it seemed our separate searches were each fueled by a prevailing feeling that we had done something wrong and needed to take measures to correct whatever our crimes were. We looked for the right ways to behave and think. We wanted to find the right priorities in hopes that the sense of guilt would dissipate. Atonement was necessary, and asceticism became a temptation. One of us even proposed joining up with the Trappistines. Thank *God* the other had the common sense to talk her down from that ledge of misplaced fervor.

Just when it seemed our self-imposed yokes of temperance were permanent, something shifted. We were at last emancipated. One brisk winter night, we found ourselves back in New York City, eager for some old fun. Although rusty from years without practice, we managed to fit our feet into some leather pumps, talk our way past a rigid doorman, and land ourselves in the center of a guest-list-only nightery. We sipped champagne, laughed with strangers, and danced deep into the early morning.

With our toes in shock from wearing something other than monastic cowhide sandals, we were barely able to walk as we teetered home along a barren West Village street. Stopping for a break, Simone turned to Ariel with a look of lament and said, "Why don't we ever do this anymore? I want to go out and feel alive like this . . . *Dude,* what *happened* to us?" We had spent the last several years so consumed with trying to do life *right* that we forgot to just *do life.* We forgot about the vital importance of just having fun. As the full force of this dreadful tragedy struck us both, we decided: *No more of this stern self-sentencing! We demand the return of our fun-lovin' freedom!*

With the pleasure principle back in full effect, we found ourselves living, once again, in the city that never sleeps. But we were no longer the fiery young coquettes we had been in the early days. We weren't interested in chasing thrills and grasping at attention. A few years of self-acceptance lessons had finally clicked. With our liberated new perspectives, we laughed at the ridiculous behavior of our younger years: the weasely men we had dated, our rigorous attempts at salvation, the idea that we needed to alter ourselves in order to be acceptable and accepted.

Doing things the way we were supposed to suddenly seemed mad, so we resolved to do only what we *wanted* to do. If we didn't like the hip club we were in, we left. If the music sucked, we danced to our own beat. If others were snobby, we were silly. Whatever it was that felt truest to who we were, that's what we did. We vowed to generate our own vibe according to our standards for fun, kindness, full expression, self-respect, and love.

A curious thing happened once we made this commitment to stay true to ourselves: We began to radiate at a high-energy frequency that everyone nearby seemed to sense. And then everyone wanted to be *nearer*—strangers, women, children, dogs, and yes, of course, men. It wasn't planned. Unlike before, we weren't in desperate need of others to confirm our worth. Our focus was solely on enjoying ourselves—enjoying our everyday life experiences as well as the inner thoughts, interpretations, and feelings they inspired. The original plan hadn't included torrents of male attention. But plans change, and sometimes you gotta just go with it.

So we went with it. Dates, drinks, meetings, and introductions ensued, but all characterized by our new approach of hangin' tough to what felt honest and real to both of us. Gone were the days of sacrificing personal boundaries or being blinded by glossy appearances. Gone were the days of tolerating abusive partners and destructive relationships. No more acquiescing in spite of the red flags flapping wildly in our faces. Self-compromise was no longer a viable option.

It didn't take long for us to notice that our new approach was totally bitchin'. Men were enamored of us within seconds. Not because we did the typical—feigning ice princess attitudes, waiting 3.75 days to return their calls, or playing a game of floozy footsie under the table. It was because we did exactly what we're telling you to do—we explored, embraced, and expressed ourselves deeply and fully. We allowed our authenticity to take the lead. We restored our allegiance to merriment and mirth, and encouraged others to join in the revelry. And that has made all the difference.

Not to say that we're flawlessly enlightened and have surpassed the human struggle. Even now we have to make the daily choice to live by our authenticity, to keep digging for deeper truth. It is an ongoing, ever-changing process that still kicks our ass on a regular basis.

And yes, it's true, we're not doctors of philosophy, we haven't yet been knighted, and we don't come from a long heritage of Native American medicine women. We can only offer you our experience and our wisdom. Which is really the only thing anyone can offer. It doesn't matter whether this wisdom is gained in a classroom, on a medieval battlefield, in a sweat lodge on the Great Plains, or on a jam-packed dance floor in Chelsea—if it works, it works. We just happen to *know* our way works, so we're giving you the best that we've got: all our secrets, all our insights, all of our radiant *Smitten* authenticity!

Above all, we hope that the journey through *Smitten* will free you to live the most extraordinary life that you possibly can. We hope you will drop your doubts, shed your shame, and dive head-long into a sparkling new sense of self. And of course we expect that very, very soon you will be causing all sorts of meritorious men to become completely, absolutely, entirely, downright smitten.

PART ONE

UNVEILING YOUR LUMINESCENCE

LAYING THE GROUNDWORK FOR MASTERFUL FLIRTATION

On the blustery Himalayan morning of May 29, 1953, New Zealand explorer, mountaineer, and wild man Edmund Percival Hillary awoke to confront one of mankind's greatest challenges. That very day, he intended to become the first person ever to mount the summit of planet Earth's highest peak—the grandest and mightiest of all molehills: Mount Everest.

This, of course, was no easy feat. Though Hillary was an experienced and capable climber, he faced extraordinary unseen challenges. The subzero temperatures, forty-mile-an-hour wind gusts, and slippery frozen passes where one misstep could lead to a long deadly drop would be enough to send most of us trotting straight back to base camp. With those tremendously treacherous conditions, Hillary certainly deserved the knighthood he later received from the queen upon his victorious descent.

Yet Sir Hillary had one crucial thing to help him overcome those extraordinary odds. More valuable than any ice pick, crampon, harness rope, or oxygen tank could ever be, he had a friend, a partner, a guide: Sherpa Tenzing Norgay.

Sherpa Tenzing was well-versed in the complex terrain of Chomolungma, or "The Mother Goddess of the Earth." Though he had never crested the summit, having been born and raised in the Himalayas, he was intimately familiar with the landscape of the region. He accompanied Hillary every perilous step of the way, making it possible for the Kiwi adventurer to realize his dream of becoming the first man to set foot on the roof of the world.

We take our inspiration from the noble Mr. Norgay, for his remarkable skill and generous spirit in leading Sir Hillary up that treacherous mountain. For the remainder of the book, we invite you to think of us as your personal sherpas—your very own devoted, expert guides, committed solely to your safe and victorious arrival at the apex of your desires. Yet unlike the duo of 1953, our journey together will not lead us over the deadly glacial crevasses of a geographical giant but instead up to the bright peaks of self-discovery and all along the cool crests of flirtation mastery.

Despite what you may have heard from various amateurish flirtation guides, effortlessly attracting men is no simple feat. You cannot achieve irresistibility through coy behavior or a put-on attitude any more than you can scale an eighty-foot rock face using dental floss and a couple of key rings for carabineers. Squeezing into the outfit and spitting out the lingo does not a successful flirt make. In order to get from here to there, just as with any vital skill, there is a learning curve that must be courageously traversed—from the inside out.

Your journey toward flirtation mastery begins here, with Part One. We start out by describing exactly how and why your authenticity is imperative to successful flirtation. Each subsequent chapter will introduce specific ideas and concepts that will assist you in discovering and discarding whatever might be inhibiting your happiness, healthiness, and sexiness.

Throughout this section, we will encourage you to explore some long-held beliefs about yourself and closely examine your behavior with men. As you move through the upcoming chapters, some of the ideas and concepts you will encounter might at first seem too uncomfortable or unfamiliar to take on. But instead of hastily dismissing anything, we ask that you approach the task with the curiosity of an adventurer. Look, examine, listen, taste, reflect. You are not obligated to permanently set up camp with any of these ideas or habits, but while high up in the mountains, you might as well sample what the land has to offer. No one really liked the dirty flavor of goji berries until they noticed they looked ten years younger after downing a few handfuls. Catch our drift? So as you move through each of the following chapters, maintain an open sense of exploration with your eye focused on the prize, and we guarantee your efforts will be rewarded.

Now, we know you might be tempted to hail a helicopter for a quick lift over this next section, to get right to the flirtation techniques. We understand the allure, but it is only by taking this journey one step at a time that you will be able to truly master the techniques ahead. So do yourself a favor and walk before you run, because we don't want you to pull any muscles later on. You are going to need every bit of endurance, strength, and dexterity that you are about to earn by completing Part One. Otherwise, you just won't have the might to trigger the avalanche of male attention that lies in wait.

All right, hot stuff. Boots laced, ponytail tightened, eye on that hunky tiger. Let's do it.

SHERPA FLASH

We may need to pause along the path and point out particular sights to take in, give specific instruction for overcoming an obstacle, or share an idea that will provide some assistance. You can think of these stops as sweet little signposts or added supplements of support and encouragement. We call these pauses Sherpa Flashes, and you happen to be inside one right now. Trippy, huh?

CHAPTER ONE

FLIRTATION'S BEDROCK

Just as a tree must have roots, a body is attached to feet, and a pyramid depends upon its quarried stone, so too is *Smitten* built on a foundation from which it cannot be separated. All ideas and concepts within the book emerge from this resilient base. The basis of the *Smitten* philosophy is, in fact, so firm, so reliable, and so unyielding that it has been deemed a *law*—the Law of Relationship. This pivotal law states: *Every external relationship is based on the individual's relationship to herself.*

This means that every relationship we engage in is a direct reflection of the quality of our inner relationship to ourselves. We reap what we sow. We are in a constant cycle of creating relationships that emulate all the aspects of how we treat ourselves—good, bad, and often quite ugly. Basically, whatever is happening in your inner world will show up in your outer relationships. This is the law. Meanwhile, each of your flirtations is like a mini relationship—a snapshot of the landscape, a taste of the treacle tart, a whiff of the whole enchilada. Just ten minutes of chitchat contains the same dynamics that will appear in a full-blown relationship. Thus the full weight of the Law of Relationship applies, completely, to flirtatious encounters as well.

Unfortunately, most of us have been misled to believe that others determine who, what, and how awesome we are, which gets us all tangled up in either trying to reach our goals of love and affection by pleasing others or by molding ourselves into something we are not. Yet, as you'll come to understand, your personal self-image and feelings of self-worth are the actual determining factors in the relationships you attract and the way those relationships unfold.

The Law of Relationship is proof that nobody has the power to deem you worthy, lovable, or cherished—but you. Whether you bask in the glow of admiration or dwell in a dungeon of detestation is in your hands. You are the sole authority of your internal state, and therefore the sole author of your romantic destiny. By following the *Smitten* way and learning to cultivate a compassionate, understanding, positive relationship with yourself, you will attract the same quality of attention from the men around you. So if you truly want to master the art of flirtation, you must first master the relationship you have with yourself, which means you must become a self-realizing woman.

WHO IS THE SELF-REALIZING WOMAN?

The self-realizing woman is the gal who continually prioritizes greater self-awareness and consciousness in her daily life. She is always on the lookout for opportunities to expand herself, her potential, and her world. She is on a never-ending mission to uncover her true nature because she trusts that at her core she is whole, beautiful, and flawless. She will bravely investigate her emotions, thoughts, and behaviors in order to better understand and ultimately free herself from those habits that cause her to suffer. She is forever peeling open aspects of her life that are not working in order to seek out healthier ways to live. She knows she is the authority of her own fate and is committed to living her highest purpose. Above all, the self-realizing woman is determined to honor her true self at any cost.

And how do you know your true self? You will be happy to hear that your true self is not some embellished, high-maintenance version of you. It is not you in your ideal body or you with your ideal account balance. It is not your most praised accomplishment or most noteworthy accolade. It is not you with a doctorate, or you being hailed as the next Picasso. It is not the events that have made up your life story. Your true self is not your identity as a Christian, an atheist, or a yogi. It is not you renouncing all your worldly possessions or the you who vows to eat only wheat germ and organic fava beans in the name of saving the planet.

The tricky thing about the true self is that it is so deep, so vast, so profound, and so pure that it is hard to get our simple little minds around it. Your true self can be described as your inner light, your higher consciousness, your wisdom mind, your authenticity, your life force, your essence, your source, the diamond in your pocket . . . It is beyond your superficial identity but not separate from it. It is beyond conditioned fears and anxieties and beyond social constructs, but still includes them in its experience. Your true self is uncontainable and infinite and indestructible. Your true self is the divine one-life that animates everything in the universe, expressed exclusively through your being, through your life experience. Your true self is your inner life force that is forever seeking to evolve, just as all life does. It is the quiet instinct nudging you forward, pressing you to expand your vision and enhance your perspective. Your true self is what shines through in moments of pure joy—when you are stunned by a beautiful sunrise or feel your heart melt when a puppy licks your hand. Your true self is expressed through love. Not just romantic love, but the swell of love that fills you with peace and contentment in unexpected and unforeseen moments. Your true self is not bound to the rules and expectations of society; its wisdom comes long before this time and place and extends far beyond. When your true self shines through, it is as if you are made of pure light and others are instinctively drawn to you—drawn to your luminosity.

The goal of *Smitten* is to help you uncover your true self and honor its impulse to shine. By letting the beams of your true nature break through, you will become radiant, and people and circumstances that resonate with your pure life force will naturally gravitate to you. As the stains of your false identity fade away, a vibration of authenticity arises. This vibration is irresistible to those around you because it rings with truth and freedom. When you live from your source, others will be drawn to you because when in your presence, they too feel permission to be real, to be free. We humans are instinctively drawn to those who make us feel good about ourselves, and nothing feels better than the permission to live from our honest-to-goodness true self.

WHY ALL THIS MAKES YOU A FLIRTING CHAMP

It is no mystery that the nervousness that comes with meeting an attractive man can inhibit the expression of our natural radiance. The first encounter/date is often a veritable pressure cooker, packed with anxiety and anticipation—a time of butterflies, sweaty brows, and loose bowels. In this state of vulnerability, it's easy to lose ourselves in the temptation to try to be what we assume the man wants us to be. Tangled in this knot of self-manipulation, we are susceptible to other traps. We compare ourselves to other women in the room, to our image of the "ideal woman" that lives in our head, and even to our dear girlfriends standing by our side. It can be an uncomfortable cycle of unworthiness and low self-esteem. Sometimes we even go cold, playing aloof and unaffected in order to mask our frustrated desire to be wanted. All of this false-flirtation default programming causes us to appear put-on, uncentered, and disconnected from the captivating light of our true self within.

Yet the self-realizing woman easily bypasses these unpleasant first encounter/date traps. She is conscious of the social terrain and avoids its pitfalls by simply trusting her instincts and allowing them to guide her throughout the evening. A woman aligned with her true nature gives off a distinctive air of confidence. Instead of calculating something clever to say, she naturally expresses thoughts and ideas that resonate with the environment. Her words and actions spring from a well of authenticity. She is in the moment, present, and alert. Her behavior is unpredictable, uninhibited, and sometimes uncouth, depending on what moves her. Furthermore, the self-realizing woman does not need a man to feel whole, so when she speaks to one, she naturally circumvents the desperation and anxiety that come with trying to fill an internal void. She's already complete, not needing to manipulate herself into some contrived image of perfection. Her behavior reflects her very real sense of certainty. Through knowing, trusting, and enjoying herself, the self-realizing woman invites others to join her in a brighter state of being, where life is just, well—better. She is open but not vulnerable. Because she is engaged, she is truly engaging. And *this* is why entering your process of self-realization will win you the title of flirting champ.

When you become a self-realizing woman, you may notice that your flirting paradigm automatically shifts. No longer are your encounters with men underscored by a focus on *his* needs and wants. No longer do you contort yourself to meet *his* criteria. You now evaluate whether he's meeting *your* standards for truth and authenticity. Understanding what honest, fun communication feels like, you set the bar for the interaction. Whether he steps up to the plate and things work out is not your concern; you honor your needs and your instincts regardless.

SHERPA FLASH

There is one other very notable perk to becoming a self-realizing flirt: The more you allow the emergence of your true self, the more likely you are to attract exactly the right guy for you. Of course it's a thrill when a small swarm of men is buzzing around, trying to secure your attentions. But it is even more exciting when the fragrance of your authenticity cuts through the fluff and catches the nose of just the right fellow. We can't always count on every single guy wanting us—sometimes the dude is happily married, or deeply shut down, or just drawn to a different type. But you can always rely on the fact that expressing your real self will make you immediately recognizable to the guy who will provide the perfect pollen to your blossom.

So make the Law of Relationship your new credo and put the relationship you have with yourself way ahead of any relationship you could ever have with a significant *other.* With this solid base, you'll never again risk losing your footing, hitting the ground, and chipping your coccyx on the rocky road to romance.

CHAPTER TWO

FUNDAMENTALS OF THE SELF-REALIZING FLIRT

As you are now fully aware, in order to become a brilliant flirt who is capable of attracting any man you desire, you must be comfortable letting your true self shine. So you might be wondering why it isn't *already* shining, since it's supposedly so *true* and all. Well, the thing is, each and every one of us has been conditioned by the circumstances of our upbringing in ways that have taken a toll on the expression of our authentic, radiant nature. We have been influenced by messages from our families, friends, and society to behave in a manner that isn't always resonant with our inner truth and that often pulls the plug on our sizzling inner light.

Although there are endless possibilities for how your conditioning influences your thinking and behavior, in this chapter we are going to focus specifically on the ways your flirtation potential has been compromised. We will examine three fundamentals that will jump-start your self-realization process and trigger a transformation in your behavior with men: Fundamental #1: Eradicate Victim Mentality; Fundamental #2: Understand Your Patterns of Attraction; and Fundamental #3: Prioritize Joy. Upon your completion of this chapter, your process of self-realization will be well under way, and you will be ready to pull back the veil and bare a bit more of your delectable true nature to all those who are eager to catch a glimpse.

FUNDAMENTAL #1:
ERADICATE VICTIM MENTALITY

Once upon a time, in a land far, far away, there was a beautiful young girl trapped high up in a castle tower . . . or way down deep under the sea . . . or chained to a rock by her father and waiting to be devoured by a ferocious whale . . . until, lo and behold, a knight or a prince in some sort of shining armor, brandishing some kind of steel weapon, gallops or flies in to save her sweet little behind. It is a timeless tale of gender role play: heroic man rescues helpless maiden.

While growing up, we are engulfed by these stories of the fragile, powerless female doomed to succumb to the brutality of the world unless a strapping young lad happens to be lured by her beauty and comes to save the day. Rapunzel is stranded in high-altitude despair without a knight; Snow White is comatose without a kiss; and the Little Mermaid is unhappily finned forever without the affections of her princely savior. Our culture is saturated with these popular tales that plant the damsel in distress in a comfortable corner of our unconscious minds, ready to wreak doe-eyed havoc on our contemporary lives.

These two roles, the passive female and the heroic male, have surfaced everywhere throughout history, media, and society. Consequently, our inner development has been deeply influenced by the widespread message that women are somehow powerless, helpless, or less than, and therefore need to be saved. We may be fully aware that life is neither myth nor fairy tale but still end up succumbing to the messages of these stories, and before long we find ourselves caught in the thorny briars of a victim mindset.

A woman trapped in a victim mindset believes on some level that others are responsible for her life circumstances. She does not take ownership of her thoughts, feelings, and behavior. She doesn't fully acknowledge how her choices and actions have helped create her present situation. She repeats the story of her pain and suffering without making the conscious choice to heal.

A woman playing the victim role is often waiting for a man to rescue her from her dissatisfactions and save her from her woes. Stuck in this cycle of passivity, she fails to act as the authority in her own life. Suffice it to say, victim mentality and brilliant flirtation are *not* in cahoots with one another! In fact, the two are bitter enemies. Playing the victim will undoubtedly obscure your luminescence and diminish your magnetism. So as a self-realizing woman, it is vital that you be on constant watch for any victim tendencies, and when you see them pop up, reach for your black velvet pouch, sprinkle them with fairy dust, and blow them straight out of your life story.

The Blame Game

One common type of victim behavior to be on the lookout for is the urge to blame. While in the throes of victim mentality, we blame others for our failures, shortcomings, pain, or sadness without a second thought. We shoot accusations in all directions: "It's your fault I'm upset! You did this to me! I can't sleep, I'm an addict, my hair is falling out, I'm unhappy. All because of you!" The victim mindset has us convinced that others are responsible for our emotional, psychic, and even physical health.

The truth of the matter is that bad things happen to all of us. Most of life's circumstances are out of our control and not our fault: loving mothers die, angry fathers lock us in basements, wicked coworkers spread malicious rumors, frogs forever remain just frogs. The outer world often does not feel kind, just, or safe, and we rarely have the power to change it. Yet this does not mean we must forever be at its mercy!

And so it becomes our responsibility to find a way to get beyond those unfortunate outer-world experiences. At some point we must stop wondering, "How could this have happened to me?" and stop waiting around for someone to fix it. Nobody else can mend our wounds. No one else can free us from the pain of past mistreatment. If we do not take responsibility for our own well-being, we will forever lug around the crushing weight of anger, guilt, sadness, and shame. If we do not assume accountability for these emotions, we will cheat ourselves out of experiencing our true, free, and liberated selves—we will become the oppressors of our own sparkle. As a self-realizing woman, it is valuable to acknowledge that sometimes life really sucks. But instead of stewing around in the "wrongness" of it all, tap your inner power and take the steps to change, heal, and grow out of this unbecoming, unamusing, and unsexy victim role.

Rescue Me

Now, of course, we cannot overlook the other crucial piece of the puzzle—no victim is complete without her princely savior. We cannot play a proper victim without expecting to be saved. It is simply part of the plotline. As children, we unconsciously absorb the message that yes, life might be tough between the ages of five and twenty-five, but never fear! Before your ovaries close up shop, you will be awarded a dashing young gent, a big white wedding, and delicate pillow shams, and you'll never have to worry your pretty little head again! Salvation is just over the horizon!

This misguided maiden role makes us think that romantic male partnership is the main thing that will provide safety and security in the world. It will save us from ever having to feel lonely again. It will relieve us of the pressure of financial insecurity and the confusion of independent decision-making. It will take away the ache of our own inner growth and let us off the hook from striving to fulfill our personal potential. It will eradicate insecurities about how lovable and attractive we are, and ease the sense that there might be something wrong with us for being single. When our prince promises to be forever by our side, our fantasy projection of what life should look like is fulfilled. We are saved from the uncertainty, the profound mystery, the utter instability that is real life . . . or so we think.

As a self-realizing woman, you can admit that this type of salvation is a myth, a fallacy, a fairy tale, and you simply don't need it. Hiding out in the arms of romantic love will not allow you to escape the world, or, more importantly, escape yourself. Searching for fulfillment in an outside source will inevitably leave you depressed, anxious, and unsatisfied. And besides, subscribing to this false idea will make you a really bad flirt. Here's why:

When you are stuck in the "save me" mentality, you are in a state of desperation. When you believe that a knight in shining armor will protect you from modern life's scorching jets of dragon fire, of course you'll do anything you can to lure that man in. You'll claw, fight, spit, lie, cheat, steal, and prostrate yourself at the hooves of his snorting steed. Without your own flameproof shield to protect you from the heat, you *need* that knight so dreadfully!

Well, you might as well get charred to ash and pray to be reborn, because you've just torched your chances at brilliant flirtation. High-intensity neediness is like a bubbling, pus-filled blister that repels all flirtatious encounters. Men can immediately sense the sickly sores of desperation. They know when a woman is frantically peddling tainted goods, even if she's doing it with a coolly composed exterior. In such a situation, a line most common in the male inner monologue reads something like

"She's just too needy," and we must admit he's absolutely right. Desperate women can be downright scary. They latch on with all their might, fearing that if they let go, they will be left alone to fry in the flames of the big, bad world. No flirtatious encounter has a chance of surviving, let alone thriving, in the heat of such burning desperation.

SHERPA FLASH

It is still possible to lure a man when playing the victim. But because this role conveys a certain message, it will always attract a certain type of attention. Acting helpless and submissive could catch his eye and trigger his desire to save the day, but this is not an ideal starting point for a relationship. If he's the sort of guy who always needs to feel needed and likes that you can't balance a checkbook, read a compass, or saddle your own pony, he most certainly has issues—which he is probably trying to avoid by instead focusing his attention on fixing you. Although a bit of dependence is a natural part of a healthy relationship, no one person should be attempting to save the other. If he carries around all of your weight, you're gonna get dropped on your ass sooner or later. No one can sustain the burden of that dynamic for long. It always ends up a lose/butt bruise situation, no matter how you slice it.

Furthermore, another truly unfortunate thing about us women when we're in a victim mindset is that we'll take whatever we can get. Because we are so desperate to be saved, we aren't picky about which knight will do the job. Whoever happens to be riding by will suffice. This inevitably leads us to compromise ourselves and our standards. We put up with inconsiderate, untrustworthy, pathetic, obnoxious, boring, classless, even abusive behavior from men because we think we need them so badly and fear a better option won't ever trot by. When we're stuck in this state of need, we forgo our power to take care of ourselves. Yet as stated in Chapter One, the bottom line of the brilliant flirt is the ability to set your standards and evaluate whether a man can or cannot meet them. You do not overlook disrespectful or inconsiderate actions in order to keep a man's attention or affection. You do not morph or twist yourself into what you think the man wants. Without this essential commitment to honor yourself, it is impossible to stay rooted in your authenticity and therefore impossible to unleash your uniquely radiant true self.

Your Own Personal Jesus

To become a brilliant flirt, you must end the reign of victim mentality and become the authority in your own life. You must place the crown atop your own head, determine to make your own decisions, and commit to maintaining your position of power. Stay attuned to how and when you might be behaving like a victim. Stay alert to moments when you feel helpless to change your conditions, to times when you blame others for your heartache or failure, or to nights when you find yourself waiting around for some dude to come rescue you from your sixth-floor walk-up and sweep you away to some cookie-cutter suburban palace. Do not relinquish your throne under any circumstances, no matter how awkward your new seat seems at first. You'll feel at home amidst the glitter of gold leaf soon enough.

With that crown firmly on your head, you will notice that you are less passive and more confident. When you make the decision to heal, you can truly re-create your reality. When you don't need to be saved by anyone, you can make choices about relationships that are aligned with your real needs and desires. You will develop a solid core of inner strength that cannot be swayed by others' opinions and is not at the mercy of past wounds. You will move from desperation into wholeness, and this is exactly the inner state that births the brilliant flirt!

So keep an eye out for that inner damsel in distress, and don't be afraid to give her the boot when she shows up twisting her tendrils and pouting her puss. Making this commitment will not only bring you closer to your authentic inner power and create more harmony in your life, but it will ensure that you'll never be stranded high up in a prison tower, legless under the sea, or strapped to a rock for a sea monster's meal. So for the sake of your personal well-being and the cultivation of that brilliant flirt within, mount your own gallant steed, draw your own prized sword, gallop straight into the muck and mire, and save yourself!

FUNDAMENTAL # 2:
UNDERSTAND PATTERNS OF ATTRACTION

Mirror, mirror on the wall, oh, tell me why he never calls? Beauty contests might have some merit if you happen to be an aging jealous queen, but if we ever got access to our own magic mirror, we'd certainly ask it something a bit more useful. In fact, we would probably go for the gold and try for the toughest question in the game of love: Why on God's green Earth do we *always* attract the wrong kind of guy? Why, when we are looking for a worthy gent, do we always wind up with a sweet-talking scoundrel instead? How come all the guys we are attracted to turn out to be addicts, cheaters, slackers, cowards, and commitment-phobes? Why do we repeatedly end up in the same kind of unsatisfying relationships with men who have less-than-stellar integrity or questionable intentions? *Mirror, mirror on the wall, tell me—how do I find them all?*

In Chapter One, you learned the Law of Relationship, which states that *every external relationship is based on the individual's relationship to herself.* This concept is the key to understanding why you are drawn to certain men. Each attraction and relationship you engage in is somehow a reflection of what's going on inside you. Your particular history, social conditioning, temperament, family dynamics, past experiences, and self-esteem all affect the relationships you wind up in. Everything that has happened throughout your life creates the criteria that attracts you to others. Your inner conditioning is like a magnet that draws in those who best complement it.

All of this would be well and good if we were conditioned to honor and love ourselves fully, to treat ourselves with the utmost respect, to treasure our creative impulses, and to support our deepest potential. But most of us have a different set of standards we absorbed while growing up that now rules our romantic lives. As if in a state of deep slumber, we never think to question why we are drawn to certain people, so our conditioning causes us to continue to attract those same types. Before long a pattern has set in, and no matter how often we change our scenery, we still gravitate to the same exact deadbeats time and again.

A key component of brilliant flirtation is the ability to recognize when you are wasting time, energy, and dazzling dialogue on an unsuitable man. As a self-realizing woman, it is vital that you are familiar with your unhealthy patterns in relationships and are able to spot the signs of a guy who will invariably turn out like all the rest. Self-realizing brilliant flirts know how to listen to their instincts and avoid repeating the same damned romantic dramas over and over again.

By becoming aware of your particular conditioning, you can finally stop seeing guys through the fog of your past habits. You can wake up to the present moment and consciously choose the fellow who will really meet your needs, instead of the one who fits into your default patterns. With your eyes wide open, you can start spotting honorable men instead of stumbling into bed with treacherous trolls. You can become aware of your conditioning so that it no longer dims your sparkle and runs your dating dynamics into the ground.

Fortunately, you do not have to dredge through your entire history or look under every psychological rock to get some solid answers. Let's leave the heavy mining for our seven little friends. By exploring just two aspects of your conditioning—your relationship with your parents, and the role you played in your family dynamic—you will likely find most of what you're looking for. *Heigh-ho.*

The Mamas and the Papas

We humans naturally gravitate toward the familiar. We continually and unconsciously find ways to repeat the relationships that we already know, mainly those with Mom and Dad (or whomever your primary caregiver was). These relationships play the heaviest hand in shaping our habits for social and romantic interaction. Roughly, our mothers teach us about women, our fathers about men. Before we are even conscious of our parents' influence, we unthinkingly seek out relationships that are in some way based upon their imprint on us.

When we ladies look for a male partner, we can't help but consider our impressions from our fathers. Dad is the guy we hold all other men up against. Our fathers play a gigantic part in what we come to expect, value, seek, and reject in our boyfriends. Dads also dictate what we think we deserve in a relationship when it comes to attention, prioritization, honor, respect, and love. Depending on the father-daughter dynamic, sometimes we rebel and choose the opposite of Dad, seeking to balance out what didn't work. Other times we go for a carbon copy, either hoping to repeat the good stuff or trying to heal the damage through our present replacement. So if your father was a covert philanderer and you can't seem to find a guy who doesn't have a roving eye, or if your dad was an ardent workaholic and your last three boyfriends all woke in the night to check their e-mail, or if memories of your old man's spotty love sends you running into the arms of obsessive, suffocating men, you are likely in the grips of a learned paternal pattern.

Meanwhile, Mom shows us what it's like to be a woman in the world. She teaches us how to feel about our bodies, our fellow femmes, and the men who enter our lives. She shows us how to attract masculine attention, and what to do with it. She passes on her tools for getting what we need from a man and for how to deal when we don't get it. She's our role model when it comes to self-esteem, self-image, and self-reliance. Without some focused awareness, it can be tough to escape the frequency that Mom tuned us into from a young age. It's not uncommon to find ourselves behaving in relationships just the way she did. We will gravitate toward the same kind of pampering men she chose after her divorce, or we will nitpick our partner's table manners just like she did Dad's, or we will find ourselves seducing our married neighbor, like she used to do while out watering the roses.

Becoming aware of Mom's and Dad's influences on your relationship choices today is imperative for the brilliant flirt. Without this understanding, you will never be able to discern why you are repeatedly attracted to the same kinds of characters. By identifying and examining the messages you received from your parents, whether verbal or nonverbal, you'll have a better shot at figuring out why you keep ending up with Grumpy when you were going for Happy, or why your guy seemed like Doc but actually turned out to be much more Dopey than you ever imagined.

So keep a close watch out for the ways that your current attractions are spawned in the conditioning of your parental relationships. Actively search inside yourself for similarities to your mother's dysfunctional dynamics. Scour your past beaus for parallels to your father's disappointing deeds. Pay attention to the messages you absorbed from their behavior or their teachings and notice whether they are aligned with your own intentions. Pretty soon your hard work will pay off: You will start attracting partners who offer the kind of union you really want, instead of having to rely on small woodland animals for companionship time and time again. Not that we don't love waking up to a sweet fuzzy chipmunk on our sill, but we can hardly expect a pocket-size rodent to be our sole company from now until the end of time.

Family Ties

The other aspect of past conditioning that strongly influences our attractions is the role that we played in our family dynamic. Every family has its own unique system, and each member has a distinct role within that system. Our roles are determined by birth order, our natural tendencies, and the behaviors we are praised for, among a variety of other factors. Every child yearns for unconditional love, attention, and care. If we figure out that we receive the most attention when we are, say, confused or in danger, we will repeat that behavior. Our role might become the helpless one or the troubled one. Meanwhile, the sibling of the troubled one might try to manage the trouble or distinguish themselves in their parents' eyes by taking on the role of the strong one or the caretaker. They then receive praise for having it together or being mature beyond their years.

Our childhood roles are so deeply ingrained that even though they were learned in the past, we still automatically enact them in the present. It is quite common to be attracted to men who will enable us to play the old role we know so well. Our conditioning has us convinced that the best way to receive love and attention from our partners is to play out the same part that got us love and attention as a child. You might have played any number of roles in your family dynamic. Maybe you were the enabler, the teacher, the troublemaker, the emotional empath, the scapegoat, the intuit, the hysteric, the comedian, the critic, the innocent, the complainer, the star, the rebel, the black sheep, or the prized hog. You could have even acted out several of these roles at different times. However, usually there are one or two main roles we gravitate to within our romantic entanglements.

So let's say you played the caretaker role in your family. You were the child who never caused any problems, always did your homework without having to be prompted, stood up for your siblings when they got in trouble, changed the subject when things got awkward on long car trips, and energetically "managed" the family system. Your parents gave you hugs for never making them worry, praised you for acing the history exam they didn't know you were taking, and generally gave an enthusiastic, nonliteral thumbs-up to your job well done. They affirmed your role, so you kept doing it. Pretty soon that role felt natural, as if it defined who you were.

So then you grew up and moved out, and now you find yourself in romantic affairs that don't ever quite succeed. Because you are not a namby-pamby victim, you decide to ask yourself *why* your love life is in such a sorry state, when—Jiminy Cricket! You notice a crucial and until now overlooked pattern in all those boyfriends: Each one was an addict of some sort! Drugs, alcohol, ciggies, sex, or sugar cookies. And then you think, *Well, of course they're all addicts who get totally wasted at a wedding, put me in charge of getting us home safely, and then pee my bed during a midnight slip of the bladder. I am still playing . . . the caretaker role! I'm always attracted to the guy who never has it together so I can be the strong one in the relationship, the one who provides mothering help, the one who is taking care of the situation and cleaning up the soggy mess in the morning. Geez, can I please recast myself already?*

If you got positive attention in this role growing up in your family, if it made you feel like you had a safe place in the household, it's not unlikely that you'll seek positive attention in that same role right now. The problem is that most of the roles we played in our family dynamics no longer serve us, and they definitely don't serve the emergence of our inner luminescence. They tend to stifle our ability to fully embody our whole self. They keep us locked into dynamics with others that don't allow room for change. They cut off the possibility of discovering who we really are and what we really want from life. These old roles are often suffocating, saddening, and thoroughly infuriating.

The truth is that these roles are a part of our experience but do not embody our true self. They're survival mechanisms we learned as a way to get by in crazy family systems and slip past stepmothers who are hell-bent on hiring huntsmen to cut out our hearts. We do what we gotta do to make it to adulthood, but as a self-realizing woman, you no longer need to play that same old part to attract the love you desire. By becoming truly aware of your habitual roles and patterns, you will no longer blindly fall into the same types of relationships. You will be able to sense when you are about to bite into another poison apple and waste three more years in the confining coffin of your past. You can now drop the old script and play the part of your authentically vibrant, flirtatiously gifted true self!

So the next time you're chatting it up with a guy you sense might be triggering your past dead-end patterns, take a quick break and make your way to the bathroom sink. If a green mist fails to rise from the mirror before you and no phantom voices emanate from behind the glass, you can simply look into your own eyes for the guidance you seek. Is he just another dud in denim? You might not be sure just yet, but we promise, just by asking the question, you will have given yourself the option to see the truth, instead of being blindly led into the dark forest of self-deception once again.

SHERPA FLASH

Although many of us keep choosing seemingly bad guys, it is important not to slip back into the victim role by acting like you were forced against your will into a dysfunctional relationship. If your dude isn't treating you well and you are putting up with it, you can't blame him. Often, because of our not-so-positive parental role models, we choose relationships that bring out some pretty ugly stuff in us and in our partners. The idea isn't to assume half the guys out there are evil, and then try to avoid them. The idea is to get clear on whether the guys you are drawn to help you live more fully, freely, and happily. If they don't, it doesn't mean they crawled up from the dungeons of hell and are awful, bastard people. It just means you have another opportunity to discern what it is about you that is drawing in such incompatible partners.

FUNDAMENTAL # 3: PRIORITIZE JOY

Before you go and burn your entire collection of *Grimm's Fairy Tales* for having implanted all sorts of counterproductive ideas into your pliant little mind, let's examine the very valid destination that each of those stories ultimately arrives at: happily ever after. Life may have sucked because your stepsisters were bossy bitches, or your pinky was pricked by a spindle that knocked you out cold for a hundred years, but eventually you grow up, or get out, and finally get happy in the end. The main problem with this setup is that it's backward. In the not-so-far-off land of *Smitten,* it is of pivotal importance to put the cart before the horse and *begin* your journey with joy.

You see, believe it or not, the most direct route to brilliant flirtation is *the total and complete prioritization of joy.* By prioritizing your joy, you prioritize the relationship you have with yourself, which is the starting point for brilliant flirtation. As you already know, if your top priority isn't this primary relationship, you've got nothing. You're like a fairy without her wand, a princess without her gown, a witch without her cauldron. Strange as it may seem, your romantic quest must begin with your relationship with *you.* Luckily, following your joy will light the path to doing just that.

Joy is the inner compass that will lead you to discover and express your authenticity. When you allow yourself to seek out that which makes you joyful, you will tap into your pure, childlike essence. This is the part of you that has always been free from any conditioning, the part of you that is wise and strong, compassionate and unafraid. It's the part of you that zoomed down the ski slope at top speed, unconcerned about breaking a bone. It is the part that spent hours setting up a backyard tea party, never anxious when the guests didn't show. It is the part of you that screamed bloody murder at the sight of a tiny black spider and then spilled giant tears when that same spider got crushed under the thumb of your big brother. Your true essence is the part of you that doesn't fret about the past or future, but exists fully, deeply, and fearlessly in the glorious present moment. Allowing yourself to prioritize joy means you are nurturing this precious inner place and refusing to let your adult self get cut off from the glittering light of your unique spirit. Your joy illuminates your highest cosmic purpose on the planet—to live from an authentic state of being and genuinely nurture your distinctive mind, heart, body, and soul.

Prioritizing your joy doesn't just develop the relationship you have with yourself; it enhances your flirtation power in another very vital way. You see, joy is the x-factor that will make you irrefutably radiant. Opening yourself to joy will infuse your actions with a spirit of freedom and play and envelop you in a luminescent energy field. No one can take this from you, no one can give it to you, and no one can resist it. When in a state of joy, you convey the confidence that you are complete, you are not trying to patch yourself up with others' attention, and the party is already in full swing, regardless of whether anyone else wants to come out and play.

So as a brilliant, self-realizing flirt, you must honor and pursue that which makes you feel wonderfully alive, vibrantly free, and giddily happy. By doing so, your authenticity will come blasting through—causing others to become immediately enraptured with your unencumbered spirit. Now, this doesn't mean that you cut out of work three times a week, lie on the beach, and don't bother with sunblock. We're not advocating recklessness. It just means that as you travel through your daily life, you consciously look for what you enjoy, and then allow yourself to be guided by the pleasure of that experience.

True Joy

This most superior flavor of joy we're jiving on is the sort that makes you feel good from the inside out without compromising, demeaning, or damaging yourself or others. It's not the ego high that comes with finding out your childhood nemesis wound up obese, or seeing your least-favorite colleague get canned. And it's not the buzz produced by high-end narcotics or lowbrow gossip, either. True joy is a sensation of deep gratitude, peace, and wonderment in being alive. It doesn't need to have a story, or even a reason. It is a swell of well-being that envelops you, opens your heart, and leaves you with a sublime sense of contentment.

Your personal experience of joy might be triggered by any number of things, small or large. Maybe the smell of a fresh-baked blueberry cobbler fills your heart with warmth, or the pounding bass of your favorite new song sends ripples of bliss up your spine. Perhaps a brisk walk through the chilly autumn woods lifts your spirits, or an afternoon spent volunteering at the local animal shelter spreads a smile across your face. Beeswax glitter candles, full moons, farmers' markets, or frothy mugs of beer—your joys are unique to who you are and should be savored without reservation or hesitation.

Take the time to cultivate your joy. Water it like a seedling, coo to it like a small pup, for the more it grows, the more you will glow. Find opportunities to nurture your joy throughout the day. Take a detour on your walk to work just so you can admire the window display at your favorite florist's. Take a krumping class instead of the usual half hour on the treadmill, just for the fun of moving a muscle you never knew you had. Sit by the river and marvel at how soft the silt feels as it squishes between your toes. Dare to start living your bigger dreams and wishes. Follow your heart toward a career that inspires you. Choose that expedition to the Brazilian rain forest during your holiday break instead of going home, where you have to refill your cup of mulled wine six times a night just to get through the bad jokes, backhand comments, and burnt turkey breast. Tune in to whatever triggers your enjoyment, excitement, and enthusiasm, and pursue it without a backward glance.

SHERPA FLASH

It is a common assumption that when you are attracted to a guy, it *must* mean it's because he makes you happy, but sometimes feelings can be strangely deceiving. If you really evaluate some of your attractions, you might notice that they do push your buttons, but not the good-feeling buttons. They might actually be pushing the addicted-to-pain-and-drama button. Or the I-worship-him-even-though-he-makes-me-feel-bad-about-myself button. Or the gee-every-girl-here-wants-him-so-I-want-to-beat-them-out button. So when you are evaluating a romantic opportunity, pause for a moment and ponder whether he provides an all-encompassing feeling of happiness and possibility, or if the high coming from him is triggering your more dysfunctional habits. Not always easy to discern, but definitely worth the effort.

Joy Division

The ludicrous thing about joy is that we often grow up fearing it, thinking if we feel happy, we'll be vulnerable to all the negativity out there. Bliss brings to mind the fool blindly frolicking through a meadow only to tumble to his grisly death over a cliff's hidden edge. We continually limit ourselves to a wary state of mind lest we fall prey to some unforeseen bad news and have to face deep disappointment or disillusionment.

Another charming lesson we learn is that joy can incite malicious jealousy. After dodging a few nasty darts during a sweetly elated mood, we generally diffuse that happy glow in order to avoid others' barbed attacks. Melancholia becomes an act of self-defense, as well as a way to avoid feeling too dissimilar to or isolated from the people around us. Since we are often surrounded by seriously stubborn grumps, our own overcast attitude is a strategy to avoid the loneliness of being the odd one out with our family or group of friends.

Furthermore, when dull despair is the norm, the experience of joy can be alarming. Being too happy might make us feel as if we're losing our sense of self or are in danger of "getting out of control." Bliss can feel so foreign that it threatens the mind's idea of who we are, rather than bringing pleasure and satisfaction. In order to maintain control of the dispirited self-image we've become so used to, we unconsciously learn to avoid joy like the plague.

And then of course there's the guilt, shame, and fear of "selfishness" we tend to tag onto happiness. We're set up right from the start to believe we don't deserve joy unless we've suffered, struggled, prayed, and pleaded for every speck of it. We must endure a lifetime of hardship to finally, God willing, attain a few crumbs of happiness before we croak. And if we do for some lucky reason experience joy on a regular basis, we shouldn't allow too much of it, or we might turn into selfish pleasure-hoarding heathens, and everyone knows that only doom, misery, and brimstone await such greedy individuals. Oy vey! The internal conflict is enough to drive a person to the brink of madness!

It is easy to get sidetracked by guilt, thinking of ourselves as selfish or overly narcissistic if we pursue the actions that thrill us the most. But the reality is that we are most productive, effective, and empowered when we're engaged in activities that bring out our authentic self. When we're doing what we love, we work the best, produce the finest product, and give the most to our community and society. Everyone loses when we deny the longings of our true self—rendering the rejection of our authenticity the real "selfish act" we were so afraid of.

Look, we cannot avoid all suffering, and we wouldn't want to if we could. The richness, beauty, and information that can be found in pain would be a tragedy to pass up. But we must not accept unhappiness and anxiety as our status quo. Joy is something that each of us has the power to access. It is our birthright to experience it just as much as any other emotion or state. Every human born into this world has the right to happiness. Not only the pursuit of happiness, but the state of happiness. Being a self-realizing woman means taking action to create and practice your personal experience of joy. Only you can do this for yourself. If you don't take responsibility for your well-being and continually leak hopeless moroseness everywhere you go, you are not only actively polluting your chances at attracting the men you desire, but you're also fouling up every environment you enter with your sludgy toxicity.

In actuality, your ongoing faithfulness to a felicitous life is the most noble and conscientious act you can engage in if you have any urge to be a positive influence on the planet. The pursuit of your own joy is the most selfless and considerate choice you can make on behalf of your fellow human beings. When you make the decision to exercise your right to bliss, you shift the world to a higher, more harmonious vibration. So the great news is that you can become a brilliant flirt and save the planet all in one shot! Now, who could resist a package deal like that?

Because your joy is so pivotally important to your process of self-realization and to your path toward extraordinary flirtation powers, we are going to assign a bit of homework here. Please start a list of everything in your life that delivers a rush of joy. Your list should include it all—from the teeny-tiny, like spotting a ladybug perched on your knee, to the big stuff, like rebuilding houses for underprivileged families. It should include material items, such as your red-sequined tennis shoes, and nonmaterial, like the sound of waves crashing. It should include people, such as your crazy little nephew who can't keep his finger out of his nose, and also events, like the annual Halloween party you plan months in advance. It should include the daily roles you play, like patient teacher to your office's new employee, or impassioned performer in your a cappella hip-hop group. You might gain joy from being a diligent organizer, an inspired artist, a joke teller, or a thoughtful nurturer. Whatever roles you enjoy embodying, jot them down. Consider all aspects of your experiences. And you might want to use a notebook instead of just a couple of sheets of paper because your Joy List should go on and on forever. Add to it monthly, weekly, daily, hourly. Make an in-depth study of what inspires your soul to sing. Your Joy List will be an invaluable resource in the coming chapters of this book—and of your life.

THE LAST HURRAH

You want the icing on the ambrosia? What you have done throughout this chapter, your courageous commitment to acknowledge and investigate the many influences that have shaped who you are, is an exceptionally positive choice to secure your own experience of bliss. By exploring your victim tendencies, the ways your parents and your family role have shaped your attractions, and your own associations with joy, you have begun to clarify and strengthen your relationship to yourself—you have become a self-realizing woman. Yes, this will bring on the torrents of male attention you crave, but it will also satisfy a deeper, more instinctual longing for personal evolution. And personal evolution provides the ultimate experience of joy.

All living things are continually compelled to grow, adapt, and move forward. It is the nature of nature to reach for and revel in opportunities to expand and evolve. When we honor this movement within ourselves and encourage it along, we are acting in accordance with the inherent flow of life. When we are in that flow, we feel most harmonious, resonant, and alive. Humans are complex beings that require personal progress in order to truly flourish. It is the nature of our internal dimensions to push toward positive expansion. And so the process of self-growth and inner evolution actually provides a deeply profound experience of joy in and of itself. Genius!

Although, we must mention that as you continue on this path of inner expansion—searching for more self-acceptance, understanding, and authenticity—you may not necessarily feel joyous all the time. Self-realization is intense work and inevitably brings up threatening and uncomfortable feelings. But the satisfaction that comes with a real dedication to inner truth goes beyond just feeling good. It provides a genuine experience of purpose, peace, and gratification that won't disappear with time, age, sun damage, or misplaced glass slippers.

So keep up the good work and don't give in to the sullen status quo. Your revitalized commitment to your own rapture is an act more powerful than we can even capture in words. As you continue to pluck out victim tendencies and attune yourself to how old conditioning has sprouted weeds in your romantic garden, don't forget to give yourself a boost of joy every now and then. Take a seat on your favorite sun-soaked rock, call forth all of your small woodland friends, and hum a happy tune as you sip a spot of periwinkle tea from a chipped porcelain cup. Keep opening your heart to the magnificent display of life that pulses in and all around you, for you are entitled and encouraged to live happily ever after. Starting right now.

CHAPTER THREE

THE LOOK

Now that you've got some solid self-realizing techniques under your belt, it is time to move from your interior dimensions to your exterior allure and explore the most dynamic *look* for the brilliant flirt. We already know that what's on the inside is of primary importance, so it follows that by expressing the essence of what's inside on the *outside,* men will have the opportunity to be immediately drawn to you. We have found that by merging inner truth with your outer look, your flirtatious confidence will soar and your radiance will beam across every inch of a crowded room.

So in this chapter, we will debunk some of the very misleading societal messages about physical beauty and teach you how to express your exquisite uniqueness through your physical form. Drawing on the creative impulses of your true self, we will explore the endless options you have to make your own statement, send your own message, and affect your own undeniable impact through your personalized look.

DIG IT

Deep within a dark cave in Northern France, the skeletal remains of an early human were discovered buried beneath layers of cold mud. Unearthing prehistoric bones is always a spine-tingling treat, but something was found at this particular dig that made the discovery extra-special. As archeologists brushed away the dust, they noticed a handful of pea-size shell beads clustered around the cranium of the long-gone mortal, suggesting that they were once strung together as some type of ornamental headband. Elsewhere across Europe, Iceland, and Asia, whorled spindles have shown up in dig sites. With the use of carbon dating, these relics have been assigned to the Neolithic Age, indicating that as far back as 9500 BC, humans began experimenting with the first woven textiles. In Egypt, etched hieroglyphics and unsealed tombs reveal the fruits of ancient apothecaries, complete with frankincense skin creams, perfumes of cinnamon and myrrh, and richly pigmented kohl makeup for the eyes. Since the start of existence, humans have been obsessed with creating new ways to titivate their form, and over the past 11,500 years, the use of clothing, jewelry, and makeup to reach the beauty ideal has evolved into a complex art.

Women today have followed right in our predecessors' fancy footsteps. We've got spray-on tans to give us glow, spiky high heels to lengthen our legs, and piping-hot wax to rip out any hint of hair we happen to loathe. By adolescence we have begun to master these tools, believing they will make us more attractive, more accepted, more irresistible to the opposite sex. Nobody wants to be deathly pale with stumpy legs and curly pubes hanging out the sides of their bikinis, because by today's standards, that's just not sexy. So we grab the pumps, the bottle, the wax, and voilà! A metamorphosis grand enough to make even Ovid proud.

But the self-realizing woman has a different reaction than most to this pursuit of physical perfection. She doesn't swallow the criteria that society spits up just because she's told it will make her more appealing. She recognizes that at certain points in time, foot binding, skin bleaching, and fastening brass rings around the neck were considered *the* methods for producing loveliness. She knows that the ideal will always shift, and she can't count on the ever-changing fashion currents. She questions the messages that are presented and makes conscious decisions about what is or is not appropriate for her, regardless of the era's tides. Perhaps spiked heels are intolerable for her tender Achilles. Maybe spray-on tans go against her environmental values. It could be that she prefers to keep hot-wax encounters limited to her Gothic candelabra. No matter what the standard may currently be, the self-realizing woman obeys her inner principles and preferences first and foremost.

This is not always such an easy endeavor, especially when you are on the hunt for the attention of eligible mates. When in the midst of a night out, it often feels as though your entire romantic destiny rests on the suppleness of your bosom and the silkiness of your hair. It's easy to worry that if your looks don't first catch his eye, you will never get the opportunity to capture his heart with your sparkling authenticity. It would be disingenuous to say that this worry is unfounded, that appearances don't matter, or that we know the secret to unmitigated physical attraction. We don't. But we do know a few ways for you to learn to take true pleasure in your appearance—to tap into the glittering bits of your inner depths and ignite a blazing outer glow. And by doing so, it's nearly impossible not to draw the attention of strangers, acquaintances, and admirers alike. Yet since the topic of appearance is so hyper-charged with self-demeaning pressure, we must begin by becoming radically aware of the toxic societal messages that have shaped our beliefs and behaviors when it comes to crafting our looks.

DOLLS, THEN GUYS

It starts early. Very early. At first it's innocent. We comb our Barbie's long synthetic hair while watching our favorite cartoon princess slip into a slender ball gown. We observe Mom obsessing over how she's "lost her figure" after having three kids as she pinches her flab in front of the mirror. We see our beloved pop star hawking some pimple cream that supposedly saved her career. At first it's all outside our reality, just images of the outer world, but before long, it starts to seep in. This is when the comparisons begin. In third-grade gym class, we're told to stand in line, shortest to tallest, just for "fun." Then things get more serious. We are made to run the mile, and are suddenly forced into fitness groups for the first time: in shape, mediocre, pathetic. By the time we're in middle school, it has become institutionalized. The hormones of adolescence have us comparing and contrasting like it's our job. "How is my physique similar to Barbie's, Belle's, and my ballet-bodied older sister's? How is it different?" Then breasts start sprouting, and things really get ugly.

By the time we're preteens, we are experts at scrutinizing our poor blameless bodies against society's ubiquitous image of beauty perfection: skinny, stacked, and stunning. We are familiar with our "flaws" and begin to brand our anatomy: short legs, chubby stomach, long face, pointy ears, small eyes, tiny breasts, fat chin, bony knees, thick ankles, wide nose, frizzy hair, big feet . . . The practice is so ingrained, the labeling so automatic, it feels impossible to love ourselves for who we are, as we know we're supposed to do.

It saddens us deeply that we women suffer so much over an empty fictional standard of beauty. It maddens us greatly that we are made to feel unsexy when in bed with our beloved because of the soft roundness of our bellies. It disappoints us immensely that although intellectually we fully understand how ridiculous this body-image ideal is, we can't seem to escape doing everything in our power to achieve it. We still devise elaborate strategies to hide our perceived imperfections, making sure our chemise covers our torso while making love, squiggling away if a hand gets near our bra clasp, and keeping a pair of shorts nearby to slip into, lest we dare walk to the bathroom with our dimpled behinds in full view. Good God, will we ever break free from this suffocating prison and fall madly in love with the flesh, blubber, and bone that carried us into this glorious world?

Yes. We believe that we can and will. But as always, it starts with awareness.

Committing to full-blown self-realization means seeking truth on all planes of our being—heart, mind, soul, and body. These four aspects are in a constant interplay, each affecting the other. If we continue to hate our bodies, our hearts will hurt, our minds will weaken, and our souls will sink. We cannot afford to compromise our health for the profit of industry or for the sake of preserving the mainstream.

So here's the rub: We don't want to fall prey to those deceptive advertising traps that hawk appearance as top priority, but we do want to celebrate the gorgeousness of our physical bodies. We don't want to feel obligated to carry out grueling beauty regimens, but we do want to allow ourselves those "enhancements" that make us feel good. We don't want to be coerced into looking a certain way just to avoid rejection, but we do want to be inspired to hone our appearance from the palette of provocative influences in our lives. We want to feel stunning and sexy not because we are told we must in order to be accepted, but because it feels good to express ourselves, to have a visceral experience of our sensual, creative, physical life force.

Our culture's obsession with beauty, youth, and dieting is so grand, and the messages run so deep, that retraining your eyes to see the exquisiteness in that which is deemed nonideal, whether in yourself or others, will not happen in one sitting. Remember, you've got a 11,500-year-old legacy to contend with. Nevertheless, for the sake of true freedom for all those who inhabit a body, you must start somewhere. The following are some suggestions that will help stimulate your visual cortex into forming new pathways for your optic processing.

TRIM THE FAT

The "fat" in your life is not that skin that bunches under your armpit (which is actually quite useful when you want to raise your arm); it is the set of untrue thoughts and beliefs about your looks that are weighing down your true self. It is the ongoing adherence to those limited judgments of what sexy looks like that obscures your real, live resplendence and stifles your actual style. So yes, we would like to trim the fat from your life forever so you'll no longer have to lug around the insufferable burden of all that bogus baggage.

Lucky for you, you've already got a head start on turning your inside beauty out and loving your looks. Why? Because you've begun to self-realize, of course! One major indicator of a woman who isn't taking care of her inner evolution is an addiction to shifting and shaping her exterior. She feels the urge to change, to renew, to have a different experience on Earth, so what does she do? She goes out and buys a new pair of mules. Or dyes her hair red. Or pierces her belly button. If you find yourself translating an internal yen for innovation into a shopping trip, you are not alone. But it's unlikely that that particular itch will get scratched with a new cowl-neck sweater.

As a self-realizing woman, you have the power to transform your physical judgments and comparisons into opportunities for

awareness and expansion. Just like you did in Chapter Two, you can inquire about your habitual choices, find the jewel of understanding in the center, and then take action based on that awareness.
So as you leaf through that fashion magazine and a harsh personal judgment springs into your path, stop for a moment and recognize the truth. No, it is not the model's shimmering bronzed lower abs that make you feel bad, shameful, ugly, or worthless. It is your *thought* about her shimmering bronzed lower abs that brings up those emotions. It is your comparison to and your interpretation of your own lower abs that sets off your reaction. Your warped assessment of yourself is the real cause of the negative feelings.

But the truth is you don't need to do eighty sets of crunches or even achieve shimmering bronzed lower abs to feel happy in your skin—you need to shift the *perception* that is creating this painful dissatisfaction. The deal with perception is that it is a personal *interpretation* of a situation, not a picture of the actual facts. Perception doesn't reflect a solid truth; instead it reveals your own inner conditioning. We've got no beef with perception, per se, but when it triggers self-loathing, we know it's time to step back and get a little perspective. Here are some of the questions we like to consider when our harsh inner judge shows up:

WHAT is making me feel bad about my body?

That model's abs are making me feel disgustingly substandard.

WHAT inner perception does my reaction reveal?

I feel I have to have solid-gold abs to be attractive, sexy, and lovable.

WOULD I expect my potential (or actual) lover to live up to this standard?

Of course not! That would be silly. I want my partner to be healthy, but also to be real—not spend all day at the gym or in a tanning booth. That'd be weird.

WHAT would I tell my best friend if she was struggling with this false perception?

"Stop! Don't get sucked into that crazy societal bullshit standard. You look amazing, your body is gorgeous, and any guy who doesn't see that is simply deranged."

HOW would I feel if I didn't perceive my body this way?

I'd feel great. I'd look down at my soft feminine little belly and love it, and then move on to more important things, like saving the rain forests.

HOW could I change this perception so that I feel good about myself instead of feeling substandard?

I could shift my thought to "The hardness of my abs has nothing to do with my lovability." Or "My soft, sweet belly makes me look like a Pre-Raphaelite muse, bathing naked by the white water lilies of a misty wooded pond." Ah, that's true. And it feels much better!

Once you recognize the outlandishness of your automatic inner interpretation process, you have the potential to stop being bullied by society and past experiences and choose to no longer berate your belly. You can be brave enough to set your own standard, right here, right now. You can look at the padding that so generously protects your precious ovaries and appreciate it for a job well done. You can be courageous enough to rip the labels from your hips and challenge your thoughts to commend rather than criticize. You can put down that magazine knowing you aren't missing much—it will all be the same stuff next month anyway—or continue to read it, praising the airbrush artists for their spectacular work. Whatever you choose to do, by picking apart your perception, you have already begun to weaken the cinching grip of self-criticism, making more space to breathe in the unparalleled bliss of true self-acceptance.

SHERPA FLASH

Most people carry a deeply dysfunctional delusion that self-flagellation will inspire positive change in their lives. They think that through constant negative self-talk they will whip themselves into a gallop and get to physical perfection that much faster. They actually believe that their critical inner voice is keeping them from getting fatter, or uglier, or sloppier. Yet the reality is that the opposite is true. Repeatedly inflicting these lashings on yourself will actually aggravate and perpetuate your "problem" areas. Emotional and mental stresses signal the body to store extra fat, whereas the emotions of self-appreciation and acceptance create the conditions that are ideal for fat burning. So if you really want to shed those pounds, look at yourself in the mirror every day and say, "I fully accept you as you are right now." Say it right into your own eyes, pierce your soul with your own love, and your outer body will transform more swiftly than that one tiny chocolate dessert vanishes into the mouths of the six women sharing it. And fortunately for you, the kind of change made through an act of love is the kind that's permanent.

Everyone has issues—some appear physically; some emotionally, spiritually, or mentally. No matter how they manifest, we are each dealt our share of quandaries to deal with in this lifetime. We propose that you let your physical issues (and all your issues), no matter what they are, be your teachers. Develop a dialogue with them; ask to be shown the underlying emotional, spiritual, and mental components to the physical symptoms. Some women put on weight to protect themselves from the pain of earlier physical or sexual abuse; acne can signal the skin's reaction to an unhealthy environment; back pain could be unresolved, subconscious rage; a sore throat could mean you are not communicating your needs. Exploring the conflict beneath the surface will often lead you to the origins of the problem and allow the physical manifestation to be resolved. By finding clarity, understanding, and compassion around the cause, and not just working to cover up the symptom, you can heal from the inside out.

Although, learning the lessons behind your physical issues doesn't necessarily mean they will go away forever. Sometimes the ultimate lesson is acceptance. But we promise that as you take steps to respect your body, to listen closely to what it actually needs, to break free of the cycle of struggling to reach unattainable ideals and then thrashing yourself for your "failure," your life will simply get better. You'll be so infinitely more attractive because you will actually like yourself. Remember, it is not your nose, your hair, your breasts, or your belly that is holding you back from finding love. It is only your brainwashed perception about your body that is keeping you from who you want to be and the person you want to be with.

Look, bottom line: Most of us are never going to attain the type of beauty that's sold in fashion magazines. Even with a million bucks' worth of plastic surgery, it's just not going to happen. We'd end up looking more like a pinched, plastic extraterrestrial than the sixteen-year-old Ukrainian waif we were trying to look like. The only thing we can do about this obvious, albeit annoying, reality is find a way to live with it. Fortunately, this doesn't have to be so impossibly difficult, because in actuality, the *most attractive* quality we can possibly possess is peace with exactly who we are. By being committed to fully embracing yourself just as Mother Nature made you, you will literally radiate the most beautiful kind of beauty possible—that of genuine self-acceptance. You needn't be five foot nine and size four with silky locks, plump breasts, and flawless skin to turn heads. Your inner glow truly is the force that can stop traffic. Again, programming yourself to see this beautiful truth may take focused effort over time, but we never said leading the evolution of our species to higher planes of consciousness was for the faint of heart or weak of mind.

SHERPA FLASH

What really irks us is how women are beaten over the head with the message that we should look beautiful *all the time*, yet we are never supposed to verbally acknowledge our beauty. We are supposed to look gorgeous at work, at play, and even when we wake up in the morning. But the moment we acknowledge that yes, we've achieved this goal and look fantastic in this pleated skirt and these alligator pumps, we are shunned for being immodest, arrogant, conceited, even bombastic in our defiance of the social norm. We are made to madly chase the beauty carrot, but if we actually catch it, we're expected to lie and say, "No, this isn't really a carrot in my hand, it's just a lowly turnip. Excuse me, I'll put it back in the ground where I found it." So when a girlfriend says how fit and stylish we look, often our reply is something like "Oh my gosh, I'm really fat today and I hate this outfit." What a convoluted waste of energy! It is exceptionally empowering to all women to stop lying about our innate beauty.

It breaks us out of this ludicrous game we are expected to play. It ends the carrot-chasing charade, because if we have reached the carrot, we don't have to keep racing after it. We are free to use our energy in ways that we choose to, not the way society dictates. So stop the bullshit. Own up to your gorgeousness in whatever form it takes, and pave the way for other women to do the same.

DRESS YOU UP IN YOUR LOVE

Now that we've picked apart some of the popular blasphemy that gets in the way of us loving our looks, let's get down to brass tacks here. The sun is setting, the night is rising, and the time is ripe for tempting those enticing gentlemen. How're you gonna do it?

By hitting the mall for a brand-new ensemble? By transforming yourself into a near-perfect copy of the latest bombshell? By attempting to expose the maximum percentage of bare flesh without tipping the scale into total slutsville? Interesting options, but we had something a bit different in mind.

You are going to begin crafting your most comely outer look by first touching base with your authentic inner interest and comfort. We want you to shift your outlook on getting dressed from intimidation to assertion. As a brilliant flirt, we want you to dress to express yourself. The following are a few key principles that can really take your outfits from passive to active expression. And what better place to start investigating your most attractive and authentic look than your very own closet?

When you open your closet door, you might see any number of things: a jam-packed jumble of sweaters, boots, and dresses; mismatched separates that seem difficult to pair; odd impulse buys that you rarely bother even trying on. Now give that mass of material another glance and let yourself see things from a different angle. A shift in perspective might reveal how each item actually reflects some aspect of you. Every article echoes a piece of your personality: your favorite color, style, pattern, season, or texture. Unless you have a personal shopper, you were the one who chose most, if not all, of what hangs on that overburdened rod. Right in front of you is a virtual visual encyclopedia of who you are.

Next, allow yourself to be *inspired* by something you see. Notice what speaks to you, what jumps out at you in this particular moment. Don't worry about whether it's in style or not. Don't even worry about whether it's practical, in season, or appropriate for the occasion. Just notice what is hooking your attention and tugging on your heartstrings. It could be a purple tie-dyed ballet skirt you wore in a dance recital, a pair of polka-dot flats from a flea market, or your puffy white ski suit with the ratty lift tickets still attached. If nothing in your closet is calling out, wander over to your jewelry box, makeup bin, lingerie drawer, or even the collection of dusty treasures that rest atop your bookshelf.

Whatever the item is that is making your soul sing, let *that* be your outfit inspiration for the evening. Your new turquoise liquid eyeliner, that dreamy coral Navajo printed scarf, a steel-gray oyster shell you found on the beach, or that pair of tight black cords your sister was gracious enough to lend you are all superb starting points for a fabulous outfit. By harnessing your deep attraction to that material object, you can create an entire look that is united with your essence. Never discount your passion for a pot of swirling teal paint or a scarf that evokes the setting Santa Fe sun. The enthusiasm and adoration you feel for *anything* is worth cultivating and celebrating. So let your sense of excitement for the cool shimmer of that Cape Cod seashell prompt a truly inspired ensemble, or allow the distinctive way those jet-black cords hug your lower buttocks to trigger a totally spectacular getup.

When you settle on your source of inspiration, ask yourself what imagery the piece brings to mind. Where do the colors, textures, traits, or history of the object take you? For example, if you are working with the eyeliner, what image does that particular turquoise slicked across your upper lid evoke? Does the blue-green hue conjure visions of the Nordic tundra, a tall fur hat, icy fjords, and frostbitten cheeks? Or do you see the slanted eyes of Scheherazade, her body swathed in a violet sari, jangling with a dozen gold bangles while telling her nightly tales? Homing in on a specific image will give you direction for piecing your outfit together. However, the execution of your image is not meant to be literal. We are not implying that you should fasten a magenta pillowcase around your waist because the Indian sarong shop around the corner is closed at this late hour. The image of that dark seductress might simply lead you to wear your hair loose and wavy, suggesting a humid, tropic Indian night. Or to slip on a few more bracelets than usual. Or to opt for that black silk shawl as a cover-up instead of the zippered jacket you normally wear. Your choices don't need to be over the top or costumey. Create a compelling effect by choosing items that subtly hint at the spirit of the theme you are envisioning.

If the coral scarf caught your eye, maybe you will be inclined to wear a soft camel suede jacket, but darn it, you don't have a soft camel suede jacket. Though you do have a soft camel V-neck sweater and cute little moccasins you kept from when they were popular in high school! Then you could go braless like a Georgia O'Keeffe feminist who just happened to throw on that sweater as she walked out onto her porch, preparing to paint another emblazoned desert cliff. Along with rocky turquoise earrings and your cheekbones dusted with bronzer (remember, you've been under the blazing sun for years), you have crafted a complete look of sexy southwestern earthy sophistication straight out of your passion for that one beloved scarf.

The point of paying creative attention to your look is not so that others will be awed by your genius ability to gain fashion inspiration from a cracked-up, washed-up oyster shell. Dressing in this way infuses your outfit with life. It lets others get a glimpse of your distinctive vibrations, the particular pathways of your mind, your singular artistic aesthetic. However high the price tag, outfits created for the sake of fitting into a trend (or just fitting in) will inevitably turn lackluster. As a self-realizing woman, you have the opportunity to flow through the evening with the sensational confidence that comes with sporting a look that is rooted in the rhythms of your true self. You've done the work—why not have something to show for it?

SHERPA FLASH

There is a thin line between using clothing to hone your expressive style and getting sucked into meaningless materialism. Fashion can be a dangerous, greedy addiction. Women become blindly obsessed with owning the latest bag, the newest trench, and the priciest platforms, hoping their spending will fill the void, stabilize the insecurity, and bolster the ego. But we know that insecurity cannot be cured with a day of outlet shopping. This is a false promise that our grossly materialistic society perpetuates. As self-realizing women, we must use our sharpened vision to see through this fabrication. We must learn to monitor our thoughts and recognize when we are stepping over the threshold from a healthy, nonattached admiration of luxurious items to a noxious, creepy fixation on getting more, more, more.

OUTFIT INSPIRATION PLAN B

The other point of inspiration we'd like to focus on is also right in your immediate vicinity. In fact, it *is* your immediate vicinity! Your body in all its uniqueness and glory can provide you with all the information you need to clothe it fabulously. The details of your features can point you toward certain styles, colors, eras, and themes that complement rather than clash with your physicality and bring your look roaring to life!

For instance, Simone has broad shoulders. For years, she lamented about how frilly halter tops made her look football-player masculine rather than forest-fairy feminine. But eventually she realized that her strong shoulders were actually an invitation to embrace a different kind of look. By blending her "masculine" assets with her softer features, she looks positively smashing in a tailored man's jacket, patent leather pumps, and a skin-tight mini. Her body's natural shape prompted her to focus on the bold looks of *Flashdance* or *Cabaret* for inspiration, rather than the flouncy frocks of A *Midsummer Night's Dream.*

Ariel, meanwhile, has feathery hair and a long, delicate torso. Somehow her natural features just sing '70s vintage chic. It's as if high-waisted jeans and ripped rocker T-shirts were designed just for her. While most of us look dumpy in empire sundresses, she dons them with grace. Head scarves make many women look like a sweaty Cinderella, but she wears them with the panache of a disco-era diva protecting her locks from the midday sun. Her wardrobe inspiration flows from the hippie/boho glam vibe her physicality is innately aligned with. However, try to pair her pale skin and lanky limbs with bright, jewel-toned solids or bold, daring accessories, and she is completely overpowered. She will quickly disappear into clothing that makes such a jazzy statement.

So follow your body's lead. Your new cropped bob might yearn for a bloodred beret, which leads you to pull out those little white gloves and the black sweater set you so rarely wear. The iridescent glow of your skin might long to be draped in glossy white silk and strands of cut crystal, enhancing your natural moon goddess glamour. The fullness of your hips might crave to be accentuated with a black fitted pencil skirt, which then prompts you to tie Grandma's green flowered scarf gleefully around your neck. Your muscular legs; your smooth, elegant spine; your sad, deep eyes; the tight curls in your hair; the refined arch of your nose; your freckled kneecaps; your full bust; the rich hue of your tan; the rosy apples of your cheeks; the ripe jiggle of your behind— they all know how they want to be adorned. Let the corporeal features you came into this world with spark your imagination and inspire you to weave a stunning web of genuine style.

When embarking upon Outfit Inspiration Plan B, do keep in mind that true style and body love are joined at the hip. This technique is only possible when you genuinely appreciate your distinct physical features, and is therefore a wonderful reason to continue to exercise self-acceptance. If you cannot see the splendor of your breasts, the elegance of your bum, or the charm of your pinky toes, you'll miss countless opportunities to create sensational looks.

As we mentioned earlier, we are fully aware that when you are out at night, it often feels that the only way to catch a man's eye is to excel within the beauty ideal. This myth is so widespread that straying from the current style standard may bring up feelings of insecurity and anxiety. But the above techniques for self-expressive style are not meant to prompt you to show up in a grass hula skirt on a windy February night in Wisconsin. We are not suggesting that you ditch all societal norms, fling yourself into weirdo obscurity, and wind up unapproachable. We are merely encouraging you to create a look sourced by your authentic self, as opposed to focusing first on what everyone else is wearing. This way you will arrive enveloped in a glowing charismatic aura: distinctive, alluring, and stunning, without being absurd.

THE GOLDEN THREAD

Before you flip off the lights and walk out your door, it's important that you actually feel comfortable in your ensemble. There's no point in putting all that effort into creating an ingenious look if you are going to enter the scene with your shoulders hunched and head down—feeling embarrassingly bare in your tube top.

Your *attitude* about your outfit is the final factor in its shine potential. You must wear your look like you mean it, not like you're
sort of into it, kind of apologizing, semi-wishing you'd just stayed
home. The confidence you emit is the golden thread that will sew
all the elements of your creation together. So if you don't feel like
you can stroll into that party, peel off your coat, and stand righ-
teously under the bright light of the foyer's chandelier with total
certainty that you look outright amazing, then that outfit is not
quite hitting the mark. You must return to your closet and make
the necessary adjustments to be inspired by *and* entirely comfortable in your design.

Remember, you are leading the way into a new time, and a
new era. Eleven centuries after this whole crazy thing began, you
finally get to make choices about your body, your appearance, and
your state of mind, and not from a place of trying to be pleasing
to men or to keep a fashion house in business, but from your own
inner knowing and your own creative impulses. Commit yourself
to practicing these principles, and you will glide into your evening
with the beauty and confidence that comes from being your own
supermodel of scintillating style.

CHAPTER FOUR

THE PEOPLE

⸻❦⸻

Unless you have particularly enticing plumbers or seriously sizzling pizza boys showing up at your door, you're probably going to have to leave home to meet the dude of your dreams (or just dudes to flirt with, for that matter). Which means you are going to have to interact with quite a variety of people as you take your skills to the streets. We encourage you to meet men and refine your flirtatious talents in all sorts of environments: your morning coffee shop, the neighborhood dog park, or the local county fair, with the sweet smell of funnel cakes floating through the afternoon air. Everything in this chapter applies to each of those scenes. But as we delve into The People, we will focus specifically on nightlife environments—partly because they are such common man-meeting settings, but mostly because people's behavior tends to be most extreme during the darker hours. With intoxicants flooding the bloodstream and sexual urges on high, you'll need precise preparation for the bizarre human behavior you will inevitably encounter during your evening exploits.

In order to have the confidence to continually express your true self, it is important for you to feel secure amongst your fellow humans. So in this chapter, we are going to teach you to recognize and uphold your personal boundaries, consciously manage interactions with other females who cross your path, and basically deal with whatever the human race throws your way.

ANIMAL KINGDOM

The diversity of life on our planet is staggering. Approximately fourteen million different species of wildlife call Earth home, and the number is only growing. Some specimens are crazy like no other, such as the Tasmanian platypus. One of only four poisonous mammals in the world, it possesses the bill of a duck, the tail of a beaver, and the feet of an otter, and is the *only* mammal that lays eggs. When first examined by British taxidermists in 1789, they were certain the animal had to be a hoax. But even with a world full of fauna as unbelievable as the Tasmanian platypus or the golden-mantled tree kangaroo or the pygmy mouse lemur, there is no animal crazier than the bipedal primate known as "the wise man"—the one and only Homo sapiens.

Said to have evolved from somewhere in Africa more than two-hundred thousand years ago, humans have developed distinct traits that have enabled us to reign supreme in the animal kingdom. Upright stance has freed our arms and hands; thus we've been able to utilize tools and create technology, unlike other species. Our advanced brains have allowed for cognitive reasoning, conscious awareness, and abstract thought, which is unparalleled in the natural world.

As our bodies and minds have developed over time, our cultural and social customs have grown in countless directions. Human beings exhibit an enormously broad spectrum of moral, spiritual, and philosophical perspectives. From the Amazonian Yanomamö's "drinking of the dead" ritual to the Australian Aborigines, who have made dreamtime their reality, Homo sapiens come in infinite variations. Basically, though we may have all evolved out of the same hot valley in eastern Africa, no two people are ever exactly alike.

This overwhelming diversity can be more than a little anxiety-provoking when attempting smooth social contact. So it is crucial that the brilliant flirt be prepared for whatever untamed social situations she finds herself facing. But before we begin to acquire these invaluable skills to deal with our differences, let's look at the one thing all of us humans have in common. . . .

THE UNIVERSAL MOTIVATOR

Gazing out over a crowd of night crawlers, it's easy to see a wide variety of attitudes and behaviors. From the cool cat leaning in the shadows to the tipsy chick shakin' it on the bar to the hungry wolf pawing at each passing tail, everyone's got their own gaming style. But what we don't see so easily is the common denominator beneath these assorted behaviors—the universal desire for acceptance and love. We've all got the same beating heart within, and from the moment of birth, we are all yearning to be held, nurtured, acknowledged, and loved. Sometimes when we are interacting with people, we fail to see this human need within them because their outward actions make us feel threatened or insecure. But by tuning into the motivation behind their behavior, you can stay secure within yourself no matter what wild antics they display.

When you realize the girl giving you the evil eye just wants love, it softens her glare. When you acknowledge that the pretentious doorman just wants love, it makes his snobbery less serious. When you understand that the tactless male admirer just wants love, it makes his manner less offensive. And when you see that you too are motivated by a desire for love, you deepen your own humanity. Seeing yourself and others through the eyes of the heart will lessen your inclination to be defensive or critical. As your defenses soften, you will be able to more freely share your true, sparkling self.

BASIC LINE DRAWING: BOUNDARIES

As you become an increasingly brilliant flirt, it is inevitable that others will be drawn in by your undeniable radiance. That is, of course, the point, but all this magnetism can result in various spatial, emotional, and sexual infringements—putting your personal boundaries to the test. As is obvious from Chapter Three, we always encourage you to display the full splendor of your iridescent plumage. But in order to do so with complete comfort and ease, you must be able to recognize and uphold your personal boundaries. This way you can strut your stuff without worrying about any of your precious feathers being unexpectedly plucked.

A personal boundary can be defined as the mark between what you are comfortable with and what you're not comfortable with. It is the point at which you move from thinking, *Yes, this is okay* to *No, this is not okay.* We each have very specific sexual, physical, and emotional boundaries. When they are being respected, we feel a sense of ease and comfort. It feels as though the other person is considerate of our space, and it is safe to be engaged with them. On the flip side, it's easy to tell when a boundary is being threatened because we feel distinctly *un*comfortable—the hair on the back of our neck rises, a knot forms in our gut, hot blood rushes to our head. We feel vulnerable, fearful, angry, or shameful. Some sort of physical or emotional warning sign lets us know that the person is entering restricted territory.

In day-to-day life, we instinctively uphold our boundaries with our energy, body language, and eye contact. Like animals, we intuitively read each other's signs and behave accordingly: *Yes, come closer; No, back off; Hmm, you're interesting; Ugh, you smell.* But there are times when people don't get the signals you're putting out, or they don't *want* to get them. As previously mentioned, this happens especially in nightlife environments, in which the levels of intoxication and sexuality are high. Daylight tends to tame our wild sides. But when the sun goes down, people often forget good manners and instead let libidinal urges lead their interactions. With your glorious tail on display, you can quickly become enticing prey to other creatures of the night.

When we are young, we often allow others—mainly men—to cross our boundaries. One of two things usually causes this. Either we don't want to risk losing the attention we are receiving or we don't know how to speak up for ourselves, so we stay quiet, for fear of creating an awkward situation. It can be easy to mistake mistreatment for flattery and difficult to vocalize our discomfort in these confusing circumstances. But as we prioritize self-awareness, we become more able to recognize when a situation is not okay, and better equipped to do something about it. No longer will we endure his hand on our thigh, his unwelcome propositions, or his attitude of entitlement regarding our time, space, and attention. Dropping our boundaries for a man's affections or to avoid an awkward moment begins to feel like too great a sacrifice to tolerate.

The act of maintaining your boundaries is twofold: It involves being conscious enough to acknowledge when somebody is stepping over the line, and assertive enough to act on that awareness. Being clear and definite with your personal edge will keep you from abandoning yourself in order to please, placate, or pacify someone else. To honor your boundaries is a deeply meaningful expression of self-respect and self-love. The feeling of inner safety you derive from knowing you've got your own back will provide the freedom for fully vibrant self-expression.

You will find that the more you uphold you boundaries, the less you'll be required to. People will sense your strength and not even bother to push or cross your boundaries. Once you do a little work in this area, the upkeep becomes minimal.

With this vital wisdom in heart and mind, let us now set out into the field to expose some common boundary-crossing scenarios. We are going to look a little closer at how to handle the pesky people who repeatedly ruffle our feathers.

THE VARIETY OF INFRINGERS

Boundary violations turn up in all different forms, from subtle suggestions to more obvious primal displays. Handling the dynamics that threaten our personal comfort can be tricky. Often a man will mask his inappropriate behavior under the guise of being friendly, laid-back, or just having fun. In these hazy situations, it can be difficult to validate our uneasy feelings and then find a way to tactfully take care of our needs. Acting on our inner truth risks conflict and a possibly awkward moment. But there are ways to honor your edge while still maintaining grace and sensitivity toward the other person.

You cannot blame the eager gent for sidling up and attempting to make contact, especially when you are in your natural state of radiance. Here in *Smitten*, we love all of God's creatures, so we try to give every guy the benefit of the doubt and be kind toward his efforts, even the clumsy ones. Ideally, we behave with poise and compassion while still clearly communicating our boundaries. Sometimes women have disproportionately violent reactions to a small offense, only exacerbating their own discomfort. There is never a need to be rude or nasty. Handling others with dignity will always make for a more enjoyable evening. So even if it gets to the point where the *only* way to get your message across is with a swift kick to the balls, it doesn't hurt to do it with a cheerful smile.

Let's get familiar with some typical infringers, and then learn some field-tested methods for the brilliant flirt to effectively uphold her boundaries.

THE TOUCHY-FEELER

Found in most nocturnal environments, this extra-affectionate mammal feels right at home with his hand resting on your lower back . . . or shoulder . . . or thigh. He has even been known to sweep the hair from your eyes, or employ remarkable stealth to snatch a sudden kiss.

METHOD: Usually taking a step to the side, brushing his hand away, or administering a small swat to his wrist will do the trick. If none of the above proves effective, you could tell him, "Physical contact is actually the *third* stage of intimacy, and since we only met two minutes ago, we really haven't even completed the first."

THE INAPPROPRIATE INQUIRER

You can recognize this hyper-inquisitive specimen by his propensity to probe into your private matters. He is inclined to exhibit a particular fascination with questions of a sexual nature, such as "You're a wild little thing—you bring that bounce to the bedroom, too?"

METHOD: You can easily deflect and redirect the conversation by commenting on his question, rather than providing an answer. Try a reply such as "Well, that's a bold thing to ask. It seems etiquette has eluded you this evening, hmm?"

THE DEGRADING FLATTERER

This warm-blood displays difficulty in distinguishing between "genuine compliment" and "crass remark." His eagle eye can spot female body curvature from a great distance, yet his subsequent vocalizations seem to lack proper screening. Example: "Wow, you've got the best ass I've seen all night."

METHOD: Instead of replying with anything resembling "thanks," we suggest no reply at all. A blank-faced stare, a slight raise of an eyebrow, and perhaps a small throaty scoff should be enough for him to realize that that shit simply will not fly.

THE SPATIAL SMOTHERER

This peculiar primate exhibits an unusually underdeveloped sense of spatial awareness. When you are continuously compelled to inch backward during conversation, or if you find your whole body flattened up against a wall, chances are you have stumbled upon the not-uncommon Spatial Smotherer.

METHOD: Like a stubborn junkyard bulldog, you must not give ground when this pushy type attempts to enter your turf. You can defend your territory by stating outright, "How about giving me a little space here, man?" But of course top it off with a friendly flash of your pearly incisors.

THE DANCE-FLOOR PREDATOR

The natural habitat of this boundary-breaker is typically in close proximity to a pounding speaker and a glittering disco ball. Identifiable when you feel a sweaty groin thrusting into your lumbar spine, sense clammy fingers inching under your shirt, or you begin to grow faint from the pungent fumes of Gucci Envy.

METHOD: Simply turning your back might work, but the more aggressive/dense of this species will often take this as a sign that you'd like him to move in from behind. Try gently pushing him away with open palms and by making eye contact, or bellowing something like "Hey! Back off, Buddy!" over the sound system. If none of these methods work, call security. He's the sort that only a gorilla-size bouncer should be handling.

You never have to allow a touch, return an unwanted kiss, give away your phone number, or let some dude take shots of tequila off your tits to keep his attention. Unless you are excruciatingly bored or missed your safari this year, we recommend steering clear of such swine.

One of the reasons we often wind up attracting guys who run roughshod all over our boundaries is that we are unclear about what we truly want in a man. Our lack of clarity causes us to be yanked around by whomever enters our arena, and we find ourselves being led home by guys who turn out to be all wrong. Because the *Smitten* techniques will cause all sorts of men to desire your affections, we strongly encourage you to get very specific about your wants/needs/values *in advance*. Make a list of all your most cherished values and the most important traits for the love of your life to possess. Imagine the quality of your relationship and the quality of attention he gives you. Then list any characteristics you aren't comfortable with and don't feel good about. Be specific. Don't compromise. Write it with a permanent marker. Memorize it. Then when you're out on the town under the influence of the sultry evening air and you come across myriad masculine prospects, you'll be able to reference that list in your mind and make an informed decision about whether he's someone you want to get to know more. DO NOT compromise. If his behavior sends up red flags on your "No Way, Never Again" list, then be honest with yourself and move on. A red flag is a red flag, even if you really want him to be "the one." By being crystal clear, you'll be able to sort through all the bad fits and recognize the man who's on the same page as you.

FEMALES

Subtle is not a word one would use to describe the male elephant seal. Weighing in at around two tons, this gargantuan mammal is loud, boisterous, and at times extremely violent. In order to beat out the competition for a harem of female mates, these guys use their teeth and ample blubber to fight, bully, and even kill each other. This aggressive behavior is typical in the male animal world—but that doesn't mean the females of the kingdom don't also duke it out for male attention when they need to. Dominant female red howler monkeys, for instance, physically shove other females in the clan in order to enforce their monogamous relationship status with a male. To show strength and rank among the pack, female African hunting dogs often kill the offspring of subordinate bitches. Though the aggression of the females might not be as prevalent, it is undoubtedly still there.

Females in the natural world have reason to fight. There are limited resources, and survival of the fittest is the rule of the wild. It's a tough business, really. Isn't it lovely that this is not our fate? With these big brains of ours, we've figured out not only how to survive, but to thrive. Yet even though we don't live our daily lives on the verge of life and death, some of those competitive animal instincts truly do die hard. If you've ever been the subject of another woman's vicious underhanded remark, you know what we mean. Those nasty little comments can cut as deep as the sharpest tooth of the deadliest great white. Women can be artful masters of passive aggression. But why, ladies, why?

Since we prefer to look on the bright side, we believe all this nastiness comes from a good place—that basic human desire for acceptance and love. We very much understand the need for attention, to be noticed by men, to be the most beautiful bird in the aviary. But it's disappointing to see women compete with one another for those things. First of all, the competition for resources is just not necessary. There is no lack of sperm in this world; there are plenty of fish in the sea. Second, beauty contests are an illusion. Other beautiful women are not your enemies. Having them around will not make you less beautiful. Third, unkind rivalry is ineffective. When you behave cruelly (however subtly) to another woman, it is a reflection of your own insecurity. Displaying that insecurity is counterproductive to your intended goal, is it not? Fourth, your hostility will ruin the evening for everyone. Throwing vileness into the air makes everybody involved shut down in order to protect themselves. The real idea is to shine bright and be an inspiration for others to do the same.

The following are some ways to handle your fellow females when the air is thick with rivalry, or to diffuse the battle before it's even begun.

When you're smacked with a nasty remark, or you sense a cutthroat challenger, it is best to recognize the root of her behavior. Again, realize that her actions come from a place of wanting love, however confused that may be. Then smile. Even if you're really not up for recognizing her humanity right then, smile anyway. If you give a bitchy retort, you have confirmed her negative delusion, so we recommend a peaceful, nonreactive smile. She'll have no fuel for her fire if you maintain your composure and emanate only kindness.

To diffuse the possibility of unwarranted competition, upon arrival introduce yourself to the other women in the room first. Instead of prioritizing your hellos with the men, aim to smile at, make eye contact with, and shake hands with the ladies. This immediately sends a message of harmony and camaraderie. Sometimes when a man introduces us to a group, he will only present us to the other men, totally ignoring the women. Whether this behavior comes from an assumption that women will automatically dislike one another, or something else equally absurd, we don't like it. It sends the message that the guys are the important members to know and the women are disposable, forgettable, mere accoutrements. We recommend making a point to counteract that particular social stupidity whenever possible.

Furthermore, when interacting in a group setting, engage the women in conversation just as much as the men. Asking the ladies questions, eliciting their opinions, or giving an honest compliment quickly extinguishes any competitive sparks. It lets them know that you value their presence and participation and that you're not only interested in generating a connection with the males. Plus, you never know—one of those ladies might turn out to be your new best friend!

These techniques will help smooth out other people's anxiety and insecurities. By entering a social scene with this open-minded, openhearted approach, you will set the mood to one that suits your heightened awareness. You can't solve the men's old-boy's-club behavior or the women's catfight tendencies—only they can do that. But you can set the standard for what *you* want to experience. Kindness is highly infectious. As you spread warmth throughout the scene, other people can't help warming up along with you.

CLOSING WORDS

To complete your instruction in The People, there is one last bit about human beings that must be understood: We have a very high propensity to take things *personally.* We have yet to hear of a platypus or an elephant seal taking anything personally. Apparently that only comes with being a person. We are not sure why humans developed this habit of becoming so offended by others' behavior and actions, but we are sure that it never comes in handy when navigating your night out.

The *real* deal is that everyone you encounter does everything they do and says everything they say because of themselves, not because of you. Even if they are really rude or mean, even if they have tailored their words specifically to you, it is still only about *them*—about their need to survive in this overwhelming world. So when you step out into the night, commit to not taking anything that happens personally. Just let it all slide like water off a duck's back, and you will be free and clear to dive right into your fantastical evening adventure!

CHAPTER FIVE

THE ATTITUDE

With your people skills now on point, you are ready for our final topic of man-meeting preparation: The Attitude. We have found that a few small adjustments in attitude when out mingling with the opposite sex can generate a huge difference in the attention you attract and the way you feel about yourself while getting it. By the end of this chapter, your new, expanded outlook will slice through any social limitations and perceived barriers, and guarantee that you will thrive in your chosen environment. Upon absorbing the five *Smitten* attitudinal perspectives, you will be totally ready for the flirtation techniques that are waiting right around the bend.

BACK IN THE DAY

Centuries before the human being became top dog in the animal kingdom, another species ruled the Earth, a formidable competitor in the evolutionary race: the Neanderthal. Resembling a shorter, bulkier human, this primitive member of the *Homo* genus dominated the land across the European continent and parts of

Asia, and for a hundred thousand years they reigned supreme over all other primates—but then it happened. A split in the evolutionary chain produced us: Homo sapiens. And as we began the migration north out of that hot valley in Eastern Africa onto Neanderthal turf, the Neanderthal populations were completely wiped out. By thirty-thousand years ago, not a single one could be found anywhere on the planet. We know what you must be thinking: "Why on Earth did we Homo sapiens prevail and Neanderthals go the way of the dodo?"

Nobody knows exactly why humans thrived and the Neanderthals died. Nobody can quite pinpoint the defining factor between human survival and the Neanderthals' demise, between human success and Neanderthal failure. But we have a sneaking suspicion that it was not due to fluctuating temperatures, a shortage of elk, or a lack of hunting agility—it all came down to one more elusive factor. You guessed it: attitude. Man's was good, and Neanderthals's sucked.

Attitude is defined as the lens through which you view life, your vantage point on reality, your orientation toward the world around you. The attitude you assume determines how you perceive and respond to all the stimuli of your environment: whether you see opportunity or impossibility, hope or havoc, glory or gloom. Antler-tipped spears are one thing, but the right attitude is the tool that will empower you to overcome the most daunting obstacles and cut through all possible disadvantages.

You see, thirty-thousand years ago, we Homo sapiens looked on the bright side of things. Instead of getting glum about the changing temperatures, depressed about a lack of foodstuff, or melancholic over the shifting landscape, we invented the party! We got ritualistic in the Upper Paleolithic, coming together in groups to bury the dead and worship our ancestors for the first time ever. We were such optimists that we even decorated our primitive digs, painting fat horses and speared bulls on our cave walls. Human survival was not by chance; we *made* it happen by taking life on with the right attitude.

This chapter is about honoring the outlook of our earliest forbearers by recognizing the vital importance of maintaining the proper attitude during your evening exploits. Though our modern-day environments are not nearly as dangerous as the Ice Age plains of central Europe, the complexities we face still demand the right perspective if we hope to successfully navigate our night out. We have distilled our definition of the right attitude down to five powerful perspectives. When you adopt them, they will cause a tectonic shift in your magnetism, generating seismic waves of confidence that will reverberate through your essence for eons to come.

#1: NO ONE IS MORE AWESOME THAN YOU

The truth is, there really is no one more awesome than you. No one. Not anywhere. Never ever. Not possible. Nope. Nuh-uh. Never happened. You are as awesome as it gets. You are perfectly whole; inarguably complete. You are exactly as you should be; you are exactly where you should be. You are a miracle. Of course, you are not robotic or faultless. You are an evolving miracle, still refining your fire-starting skills and experimenting with the best methods for skinning deer. Yet to acknowledge your pure primal awesomeness—despite any areas you may still be cultivating—is a poignant expression of self-love. Unconditional self-love is integral to grasping this principal and reaping its rewards.

When you know that no one is more awesome than you, instead of surveying the crowd to judge how you match up in looks, coolness, or brute strength, you feel uniquely beautiful and exceptionally secure. When you walk into a room, or a meadow, totally digging yourself, others immediately get the message that you are someone special. They sit up and take notice of you. They are intrigued by your confidence and kindness, and want to move in and bathe in the warmth of your solar glow.

Whereas if you enter with the attitude that you're beastly, unworthy, or dull, others get that message and assume it's the truth. Remember, you are a stranger to them; all they can do is read the signs you are emitting. Your level of magnetism is in your hands. You can decide to own your awesomeness and draw others in, or reject it and essentially lie to everyone you meet. Oh yes, it is a lie to imply that you are un-awesome when you are clearly totally awesome. Even if it's a nonverbal, subtle energetic transmission, it's still a lie.

SHERPA FLASH

This principle is not "you are more awesome than everyone else." We do not advise you to act superior, assuming others are beneath you or unworthy of your presence. It is well known that an attitude of superiority is really a mask for deep feelings of inferiority. Most humans have these feelings of inferiority stemming from childhood. Instead of doing the work to overcome those feelings, they take on a superior attitude. It's like a psychic quick fix. However, this is not recommended and is not a core principle of the right attitude for the brilliant flirt. Some onlookers might be momentarily mesmerized by the sheer audacity of snobby superiority, but the effect won't last long, for it is not built on authenticity. Instead we ask you to trust that there is no sliding scale of awesomeness; we are all worthy and deserving of love, attention, and a chance to shine.

Why is it that we women have such a difficult time owning our awesomeness? Why do we downplay ourselves, acting modest if another points out our beauty, talents, or success? We're given the message that we must be gorgeous and accomplished to be worthy, but we rarely take even a moment to appreciate those qualities in ourselves. We always seem to focus on what we lack— still a little too pudgy, a little too broke, a little too lonely, a little too neurotic. Owning your total awesomeness means you recognize, praise, and love yourself *now.* Celebrate the victories you've *already* achieved, appreciate the abilities you *already* have, honor the beauty you *already* possess—without modesty or self-deprecation. Without immediately moving to counter it by saying, "Yeah, but that was no big deal." Do it fully. Own it completely. Eat yourself up till there's not one morsel left. This is the way to create more and more of the things you want.

Look, even if she is stunning supermodel material, she's not more *awesome* than you. Even if he summers in Sweden and winters in Vail, he's not more *awesome* than you. Even if she started her own business and is a billionaire at twenty-five, she's not more *awesome* than you. Even if he just shot the cover of your favorite nature magazine and travels the world seeking out new species of wild orchids, he's not more *awesome* than you. Even if her cocoa skin is spotless and her hourglass figure is flawless, she's not more *awesome* than you. Even if she is a famous movie star dating the hottest guy in Hollywood, she's not more *awesome* than you. Even if she can recite all the U.S. presidents in order, knows the function of mitochondria, and can name all the major battles of the Crimean war, SHE'S NOT MORE *AWESOME* THAN YOU.

So—your being awesome does not mean others are less awesome. And when others are awesome, it doesn't mean you are less awesome. It just means everyone gets to be awesome! What's more, beyond knowing that you are awesome, this principle is all about knowing that *life* is awesome. Self-love is life-love. Which is indisputably—yes—awesome.

#2: BE REAL

This principle is about committing to an attitude of honesty, of being real about your perceptions, instincts, thoughts, and feelings. If the cabby's driving is causing your palms to sweat and your bowels to gurgle, tell him about it. If your feet are asking you to wear flats instead of heels, do it. If your gut says to not get into the limo with that crew of drunk D-list celebrities, don't. Have the attitude that what you perceive, what you feel, is real. Then make honoring your real feelings top priority in all aspects of your night out.

This principle allows you to be sensitive to your own needs, and also asks that you be honest with those around you. As we saw in the previous chapter, you will encounter quite an array of individuals, both men and women, throughout your night. As you interact, you will naturally pick up on clues about each person's character and integrity. Being real means you honor these perceptions and act accordingly.

For example, a couple of cute males saunter over to you and your female companions, introduce themselves, and begin conversation. During the interaction, the guy you have your eye on drops a subtle comment implying that your girlfriend's opinion on the new economic stimulus bill was "cute" and you are caught off guard by the misogynistic undertone. Instead of letting it slide because you would rather not have it interfere with your feelings of attraction, being real means that you acknowledge the offense you felt and either speak up or split. Whatever your action, when you are being real, you don't shuffle off your inner knowing and just let it slide. As a self-realizing woman, you know that being real is more important than stony silence, regardless of how much you wanted him to be the right guy.

So if you spill your soda and he doesn't move one muscle to help mop it up, if you sneeze and not even a mutter of "gesundheit" leaves his throat, if you've been chatting together for forty minutes and he hasn't asked more than two questions about your life, be real with yourself about what these signs indicate. If you sense he's not quite the generous gentleman you need, don't deny it; accept it and gracefully move on. Remember, as a brilliant flirt, you do not force yourself to take the sub-par deal he's offering. Know your values, set your standards, and really detect if others can or cannot meet them.

Sharing these real observations and practicing interpersonal transparency with those around you will more often than not work in your favor. Others will appreciate your self-trust and courage to communicate directly. It will give them permission to be more real as well. So you might say, "Since you keep looking around the room, I'm getting the sense that you're not very interested in this conversation. Is that the case?" or "I'm concerned that my comment about your vegetarianism may have hurt your feelings. Is that so?" By vocalizing your perceptions, you give the other person the opportunity to state their side of the story and forge the way for more honest communication.

Unexpressed feelings and thoughts build agitation, which leads to suspicion, judgment, and disconnection. Better to just find out what's happening or let the other person in on what's happening with you. So if your friend's snarky comment about your inability to properly boil a field pheasant triggered you to flare up and declare that she couldn't pressure flake a piece of flint if her life depended on it, don't pretend everything is fine. Let her know her words bruised, and then apologize for attacking her. Even if transparency makes things a little hairy for a good three to seven minutes, it's better to tolerate that awkwardness than go through the whole evening acting shut down or passive-aggressive because of built-up resentment. Expressing the truth—being real—will always lead to richer, more nuanced, more comfortable connections.

Being real means honestly following your inner urges for fun as well. Maybe you have the impulse to go rock out even though no one else is on the dance floor. Maybe you have the sudden desire to talk to the funny-looking fellow at the end of the bar. Maybe you feel like proposing a dare to climb up the fire escape and howl at the moon. These impulses are real, and by following them, you allow your inner creativity to craft much more thrilling evening experiences.

Being real can take some getting used to. In the effort to remain socially acceptable, we lose our inner connection with our gut impulses. In the hope of avoiding uncomfortable feelings, we pretend to see in others only what we'd like to see. Yet soon after you begin practicing this technique, you'll find that saying what is truly on your mind, articulating your real feelings, and behaving how you actually want to will make your evening so much more satisfying that you'll never throw your authentic expression to the wolves again.

#3: ALL-INCLUSIVENESS

Those first early human get-togethers were most likely intimidating scenes. Without any practice at preschool or prom, our ancestors were faced with the awkward task of mingling. Who's invited over to the cave; who's not? Whose bear hide pelt is the prettiest; who's got the rattiest piece of fur strapped to their back? Whose frontal lobe has developed a sense of humor; whose hasn't quite caught up in the evolutionary race? Socializing today can be no less daunting. Even the most popular among us are usually just as plagued by the fear of being an outsider as those who regularly find themselves on the fringe. The self-realizing woman is aware of this social insecurity in others because she is aware of it in herself, and she knows it's not cool to leave anyone out in the cold. She refuses to take part in making anyone feel like an outcast and aims to generously open her arms to all. So she hones the attitude of all-inclusiveness—the attitude that we are all equal and deserving members of the tribe.

The attitude of all-inclusiveness is that of the bountiful host who invites everyone to the banquet. It is the attitude that there is plenty to go around, and if someone is left out, everyone misses out. It is the attitude that has us initiating a reseating shuffle and saying, "Of course we can squeeze in a few more chairs here" to the two ladies standing sheepishly over in no-man's land. Or has us saying, "Hey, what're *your* thoughts on putting orangutans in space?" to the quiet, cross-eyed guy at the other end of the table. As a self-realizing gal, you've got the backbone to drop the attitude of social survival of the fittest and instead actively include and engage everyone who hopes to join in the feast.

By adopting the attitude of all-inclusiveness, you will generate comfort within the group. People will naturally relax their defenses when they know they are invited and included. With this attitude, you will draw people out of themselves and spark an atmosphere of good cheer. Nobody has fun when there is an odor of segregation and exclusion in the air. We unconsciously pick up on the fact that although we might be socially safe right now, at any minute we could become the scapegoat of the party. This dynamic creates a permeating anxiety that hangs over the scene, stomping out the possibility of unfettered merriment. That's why it is such a divine relief when someone takes the reins and sets a tone in which everyone is welcome, everyone is honored, and everyone is treated with care and respect. Become a master at promoting social justice, and your evenings will be filled with the unparalleled love of loving humanity.

#4: NONATTACHMENT

The only thing we can really count on in life is that we can't count on anything. When we make the decision to walk out our front door, there is no way to know what we'll encounter once we hit the street. No matter how hard we plan or how much we try, the world just doesn't behave how we want it to. The world doesn't really care that you wanted to get a tan; it sends rain clouds anyway. Or that you wanted to make your flight; it throws construction across the road anyhow. Or that you were dying to catch sight of a saber-toothed tiger; it plunks a large woolly mammoth right in your path instead. So in order to free yourself from expectations that could create disappointment on your night out, we are encouraging you to practice an attitude of nonattachment.

Nonattachment is widely acknowledged as one of the most powerful ways to transcend daily agitations and restraints. When you cling to hopes and ideals for any situation, conflict arises in your system because you are resisting *what is* actually happening. But by practicing nonattachment, you begin to accept and allow *what is* instead of fighting it. This way whatever you encounter, you can just go with it. Sometimes you go into it, and sometimes you get out of it, but whichever way you choose, you must work with what's really in front of you—not what you think should be in front of you. Clinging to expectations will narrow your world.

By rolling with what is actually happening, you will avail yourself to make the best of any possible scenario.

So abandon your hopes and dreams. Sure, head out there intending to see everything work out, but also know it could all be a total flop. You might stride into that nightclub glittering and glowing, ready to take on the night, only to find a sad old brute slumped over the bar and a bitter back-alley waitress scowling in your direction. Or maybe the place will be so packed that you can hardly breathe, and you get squeezed back out the entrance before barely getting a toe in. It's not at all unlikely that your destination of choice will disappoint, but that's part of the adventure—seeing what the world is going to serve up and rolling with it. If you approach your evening with an open-minded, attachment-free sense of humor, it is less likely that you will be disappointed if things don't turn out quite like you imagined when you were back home blowing out your bangs and beefing up your bra.

Though it is comforting to believe we are in total control of our own fate, sadly, we are not. There are countless forces at play that shape our experiences and destinies, and we have little say in how it will all play out. But we do have a say in how we will handle each circumstance as it comes—with grace, humility, resistance, or rage. Through an attitude of nonattachment you can let go of any attempts to control or manipulate your fate. As you surrender yourself to the unknown, the unpredictable, and the uncontrollable, you are filled with an easygoing trust that the world will provide you with *exactly* what you need. So let go of your evening expectations and know that though you may *think* you want a fierce, strapping tiger, sometimes a hulking, shaggy-haired, elephantlike creature is actually what you need the most. Nonattachment will always show you the beauty in the unexpected beasts of life.

#5: ANYTHING IS POSSIBLE/EVERYTHING IS NEGOTIABLE

We are not in control of our fate, but that doesn't mean we can't ever have what we want. Quite the contrary: *Anything* is possible. This attitude is about knowing that when you step out into the world, you really can be, do, and have whatever it is you desire. The blocks you perceive in your mind do not necessarily exist. When you have the attitude that anything is possible/everything is negotiable, you never have to take no for an answer.

This perspective means that the fulfillment of your wants is completely possible, no matter how bleak the situation appears. Instead of seeing all the ways you cannot have something, you advocate for yourself and fight for what you desire, regardless of the rules and regulations. It might be that you have a taste for a free glass of champagne, entry into a red-carpet event, or would like to find a way past the rusty old gate that's keeping you from exploring an abandoned estate. Whatever it may be, as soon as you hear yourself say or think it is impossible, ask, "Is that true?" No, it's not true, so go about thinking up ways to get it! Have the ingenuity of a budding inventor, the resourcefulness of an ensnared secret agent, and the boldness of an audacious, fresh-faced teenager. You will be surprised how much the world responds to a little jazz, spit, and a smile.

Often we avoid negotiating because we're afraid to push, ask, or argue. We are scared we might be rejected or be told we're "causing a problem." So when we hear "no," we squeak out an "okay" and meekly drop the case. Women especially are taught to agree, so we tend to acquiesce at the first sign of resistance.

But the attitude that anything is possible/everything is negotiable means you toss aside your gender-based conditioning and use your powers of reasoning to make a real, smart, honest effort at getting what you want. You might ask the host exactly why your party cannot sit at that table if the room is half-empty. Why is that the policy? How can you work it out together? Just because someone made up a rule, that doesn't mean there is a good or even a logical reason for it. Discover what is stopping that person from granting your wish and then find a way to make it pleasurable for them to change their mind.

Be genuine, kind, gracious, playful, and respectful, but also persistent. Smile while stating your case honestly, eloquently, and lightheartedly. Make it a win-win situation. Nobody has to be the loser, risk their job, or endanger their life. So you might say, "Hmm, twenty dollars? That's a little out of my nightclubbing budget—how about a hot fiver instead?" Or "Ah, yes, I did hear you say that it's invitation-only, but I would so love to shake it with this crowd. I guarantee no one will be disappointed by my presence!" (Because nobody is more awesome than me!) By asking for exactly what you want, you are giving that person the opportunity to make you feel good. You are giving them the opportunity to satisfy you, to be a champion of the everyday peoples. So when they *do* grant you your wish, be sure to praise, thank them profusely, and show them how happy they've made you. Make them feel good for making you feel good, and everyone will feel great for having beaten the system.

When you are not attached, you can risk asking for exactly what you want—if it doesn't work out, so be it. Who cares? No big deal. Your self-worth is not wrapped up in whether or not you get into a party, get the table you like best, or get to sleep in the coolest corner of the cave. The point of this perspective is to know that what you want is possible, so stretch yourself and go for it. As you take on these kinds of low-risk challenges, the world looks less rigid, the night is less predictable, and you infuse your life with the thrilling spirit of possibility.

THE CULMINATION

Armed with the right attitude, we have no doubt that you've got what it takes to migrate across Earth's seven continents, build the foundation of human civilization as we know it, or just have a really good Saturday night. There is no glacial divide too big or cognitive processing leap too great to stop you now. With Part One under your pelt and your luminescence on high, you have officially rendered yourself unstoppable. Go, now, little Homo sapiens, to the eight Earth-shattering flirtation techniques that lie in wait.

PART TWO

THE WAY OF THE BRILLIANT FLIRT

THE 8 EARTH-SHATTERING
FLIRTATION TECHNIQUES

As we pause here together on the threshold of flirtation mas-tery, let us take a moment to reflect upon the brave journey you have taken thus far. You have extricated your victim behaviors, overhauled your relationship perspectives, and tapped into your wellspring of joy. You have come to respect your body, craft a look derived from your essence, uphold your personal boundar-ies, and take on a winning attitude while out on the town. Now as we confront the final leg of our journey, it is safe to say that you are fully prepared to collect the priceless booty you came for: the ability to render any man thoroughly enthralled with your sparkling, divine essence at very first flirt. *Oh, yeah . . .*

Flirtation mastery feels amazing. Sure, it's great to feel like the most breathtaking bird in the aviary and garner tons of male attention, but that's not actually what feels the best about being a brilliant flirt. What really feels the best is receiving this affection but not *needing* it. If you recall from Chapter One, the self-realizing woman is a top-notch flirt because she does not depend on a man to feel whole; she knows she is already com-plete and therefore circumvents the desperation and anxiety that come with trying to fill an internal void. She is aligned with her true nature and exudes a distinct air of confidence. She trusts her instincts and allows her truth to guide her throughout the evening. Therefore she attracts all the men she desires without ever losing touch with her own inner compass.

The point is that these eight techniques won't mean jack if you do not stay in your process of self-realization. So even when we are no longer riding your heels, continue to cultivate an exploratory relationship with your feelings, thoughts, experiences, and behaviors. By staying rooted in your personal commitment to living truthfully, these techniques will naturally emerge from an authentic place and be genuinely effective, rather than contrived. Remember, as a self-realizing woman, you aren't in the business of anticipating what he may or may not want from you. You are simply functioning honestly, following your impulses, and living by your standards. Always. Whether he can or cannot meet you in that place of authenticity is up to him.

The eight techniques ahead should be thought of as guidelines for the expression of your own innate flirtatious instincts. As such, they are not meant to be heeded word for word. As your devoted sherpas, we do not want you to follow exactly in our footsteps; we merely hope to set you striding in the right direction: up, up, and away, beyond our own experience and expertise. We want you to gather up all our teachings, tuck them away in your rucksack, then wave goodbye as you forge along your own glorious path out across new plateaus, peaks, and valleys of flirtation excellence. So please do not take any specific instruction as the law of the land.

The only thing that should be considered a concrete principle is the spirit behind each technique: *full and honest expression of who you truly are.* With this principle firmly in your grasp, there is no saying the wrong thing, revealing too much, revealing too little, or messing up. If you feel you said the wrong thing, you could say, "I feel I just said the wrong thing," and then it's no longer the wrong thing to have been said. You can always trump anxiety with truth.

As you metabolize this message and begin to activate the techniques, you'll find that you quickly become the enticing temptress you were born to be. Like an opium den mistress, your quarters will never be empty. But instead of offering illicit brown powder from an orange poppy pod, you'll be doling out spoonfuls of your purest essence, leaving each visitor to chase your white dragon of truth over all terrains, never wanting to lose sight of the genuine goods you've got to give.

The time is now upon us to set off to the pinnacle of mastery. Pick up and stow away each and every technique along the path. Hold them in your care until you truly grasp their meaning, until you have assimilated their spirit into your own. Then gather them up and toss them over a cliff, letting them scatter and crash into the ravine below. Listen to your impulses and allow your own talents to guide you through every aspect of your night, morning, and afternoon out. For this is the way of the brilliant flirt . . .

SHERPA FLASH

One important topic that must not be overlooked is how and where you will meet eligible gentlemen with whom to practice the forthcoming techniques. In a nutshell: anywhere and everywhere. A hot dog stand, the local coffee shop, a running club, a yoga studio, a baseball game, a karaoke bar, at work, at school, at a Fourth of July barbecue, on jury duty, on a blind date, online, at a gas station, at happy hour, at a sushi bar, at a dive bar, through a friend of a friend, on the subway, at your church, at your mosque, at your temple, on an airplane, or on the peak of a mountain you've just crested after a long, exhausting hike. These techniques are to be implemented *everywhere*. But in the interest of increasing your odds, we do recommend continuing to widen your circle by saying yes when you're invited to a random party, by signing up for a six-week astronomy course on a whim, or by taking your lunch break out in the park instead of cloistered in your cubicle. Look for opportunities to go out among humanity and enjoy yourself, and mankind will surely perk up and take note.

THE QUIRKY QUESTION

You shoot him a sideways glance, he slides into your orbit, and you say,
"So what's your favorite subway stop?"

Here it is, the first moment of the first encounter, and it'll be gone faster than a blazing comet vanishing into the midnight sky. In this fleeting instant, there's no time for humdrum how-do-you-do's that fail to incite an initial spark of intrigue. So the very first technique will show how posing a quirky question right off the bat will quickly entice the attention of a suitable gentleman by cracking open the conversational possibilities in a most dazzling way!

"Where are you from?" "What do you do?" "Do you come here often?" Blah, blah, and blah! A generic question will almost guarantee a predictable, forgettable response. *Oh, here we go again,* sighs the mind, *right back to that same old ring-around-the-rosy of getting-to-know-you jargon.* You see, the opening moments of a first encounter can either rocket the repartee into cosmic fascination or dump it into a crater of mind-numbing monotony. The choice is yours. But by seizing control of this technique, we guarantee that you'll never run the risk of drowning your dialogue in a pit of platitudes again!

Your quirky question can arise at the outset of the encounter or emerge after an exchange of initial introduction. One ideal placement for your question is in the lull after the hellos and before the boring conversation topics potentially set in. When crafting your quirky question, you don't want to sound so out of the blue that he thinks you've just escaped the booby hatch. To start, simply take a look at your environment, notice something that catches your attention, and then proceed with playful curiosity. For instance, if you're mingling in a sports bar, you might ask him to name his all-time favorite athletic news commentator. If attending a poetry reading, perhaps query whether he's had any good revelations on the nature of the cherry blossom lately. While mixing it up at a political rally, you could challenge him to pick the celeb who would make the *worst* possible Secretary of State. Or if the environment doesn't spur any specifics, just go random. "Where does your joy come from?" "If you could have any job in the whole wide world, what would it be?" "What's the most miraculous thing you've seen today?"

This style of questioning will boost the encounter into Technicolor. Don't worry if your query is strange or new; the point is to hook his imagination instead of his rote response. He might be caught a bit off guard, but your dynamic will immediately spring to life as he realizes he's not dealing with any old run-of-the-mill madame. The difference between asking, "Do you come here often?" and "Do you believe in ghosts?" spells the difference between a tedious two-minute exchange and endless opportunity for genuine engagement.

But don't be quirky just to be quirky. Your authentic curiosity is the crux of this technique. By asking a question that you are actually interested in, you expose your unique perspective and therefore bare your true self. This is the beginning of a brilliant encounter. Conversations that emerge from creative questions have a funny way of diminishing self-consciousness and amplifying laughter and delight.

If reading these last paragraphs has you quaking in your boots at the thought of actively flirting with a man you are interested in, you're not alone. We know how frightening it can be to try to connect with a guy your heart is all aflutter over. So here's our easy fix: Pretend you are just talking to a buddy. Act as though he's the kid next door and you're just having a nice neighborly chat. Give the impression that you're not necessarily looking for a romantic or sexual connection. Acting casual at first will give you a chance to catch your breath and slow down your heartbeat. Once you've gathered your wits and become confident that you've got his full attention, you can then let on that your interest is in more than just a friendly game of kick the can.

ORIGINS

This technique harkens back to the days of childhood when we'd make new friends by asking, "What's your favorite color?" or "If you could be any animal, what would you be?" or "What super power would you want most?" Discussing the merits of pink versus purple, the pros of galloping like a horse versus trolling like a shark, or the advantages of flying at hyperspeed versus shooting fireballs from your fingertips never got old back then. Take a cue from the kid in you and dare to make your adult chatter sing with that same vibrancy and charm!

We understand that it can be nerve-wracking to ask a cute stranger, "If you had to trade hairdos with anyone in this room, who would you choose?" But this technique is less about the question and more about the tone you are setting. It is about defying the first-encounter patterns that have become all too familiar.

By posing a quirky question, you are throwing a wrench in the usual and cracking open the unpredictable.

So if he doesn't get it at first, don't be too concerned. We've found that some guys will immediately latch on as though they've been thirsting for a juicy chat for years, and others will be momentarily perplexed. If he's the latter type, no worries; just contextualize your question a teeny bit and ask it again. "Well, there's a rumor that this tavern is haunted by an old man who died a gruesome death in the apartment above, but I'm not sure I believe in all that—what do you think? Are there ghosts drifting among us?" Just act like it's the most natural thing in the world, and see what happens from there. He'll most likely catch on quickly and before you know it, you'll be deep in discussion about the creepiness of mausoleums or your dabbles with exorcisms or his near-death experience while handling an electric lint remover— all much more interesting than trading fine's and cool's and not really's for ten minutes, then escaping to the bathroom for the sole reason of putting your mutual awkwardness out of its misery.

Your conversation-starting courage showcases your confidence, daring, and playfulness—which are all *super* sexy. Furthermore, it will provide a glimpse into your universe, into the particular ideas that you notice and ponder. Asking a quirky question may seem like a superficial "technique," but it cuts much deeper. Through this method, you offer bits of your very special perspective on life and reveal your wildly magnetic and thoroughly rare streak of curiosity. Upon posing your original query, watch his focus shift exclusively in your direction as he realizes that an exceptional creature has entered his stratosphere.

Upon asking a man a quirky question, if he should be at all unkind or critical, this is very good information. Every once in a while, a guy who looks perfectly friendly and attractive will turn into an ogre if you venture off the beaten social path. Maybe it's because he's a control freak, or maybe it's because he is just seriously jerkish, but if this should happen, we recommend making a graceful departure ASAP. A friendly smile and a "never mind" along with a pointed walk in the other direction are perfectly acceptable actions to take when faced with such cretinish behavior.

GET HIS SHINE ON

This bold move is especially effective because it invites *both* of you to shine. People love expressing their unique selves. By asking a specific, imaginative question, you give voice to your creativity while also providing him with the opportunity to present himself in an original, genuine way. All that any of us really wants is to be acknowledged and appreciated for our individuality. By inviting this dynamic right from the get-go, you are sending the message that with you, the sky is the limit; with you, he is welcome to open up and share himself fully; and with you, he's going to have out-of-this-world fun no matter which topics you come upon or locales you stumble into.

Ariel first discovered the power of this technique in a downtown pool hall one evening. Check it out:

While chalking up the end of her stick, Ariel noticed a stubbly stud at a neighboring table who was giving off "I'm a loner" vibes in spades. But his back-off attitude didn't dissuade Ariel;

she couldn't resist the guy's brooding allure. So between games, she casually perched herself on a stool next to his. After a brief hello (to which he barely grunted a response), Ariel took a sip of her beer, slanted her eyes in his direction, and asked, "What makes you feel really alive?" "Huh?" he replied coolly. She asked again, "What in life makes you feel really, truly alive?" The long pause that followed caused her to wonder for a moment if she had crossed a line with this sullen fellow, but then he started to smile. "I like fishing," he said. "Spending the day out on the water, away from everything . . . But the best part is when we get the first good catch of the day. Right then, just as it dies, we each cut a piece off and take a bite." "You take a bite out of the raw, uncooked, dying fish?" Ariel asked, and the guy broke down laughing. "Yeah, I know it sounds weird, but it just, well, it's kind of a ritual, and it feels like an act of respect, you know?" Ariel was completely charmed by this strange man with the radical fishing rituals, and by the end of the next game he had dared her to come over to his place for a bite of the freshest fish in town.

One of the best things about asking a quirky question is that the guy's response will give you significant information about who he is. He will invariably reveal truths about himself that might normally take light-years to find out. You will learn how open-minded, thoughtful, resourceful, spontaneous, and willing to connect he actually is just by throwing out an unpredictable query. You will be able to see his comfort level with adventure, how he handles unexpected situations, and whether he is too self-conscious to play freely. Sometimes a guy who seems too cool for school is actually just a bit shy, and your kind-spirited question is precisely what he needs to come out of his shell. Other times it turns out that the man oozing sex appeal can't handle a creative thought, and you've just saved yourself oodles of flirtation energy. A quirky question or two is the perfect way to swiftly determine if he's operating on your wavelength or if he's vibrating on a totally different frequency.

When shaping your inquiries, be sure you aren't setting the stage for a nasty or negative conversation. We don't want to insult anyone; we want to keep it light, playful, and maybe a little profound. Using your surrounding environment or referencing a bit of pop culture is a great way to ensure that you are both in the loop, but be careful that you aren't trashing others along the way. We all know that certain celebrities or politicians are ridiculous, but bringing criticism into a fresh relationship will inhibit its growth. Stay positive, or focus on how something is silly, rather than stupid. Also, avoid getting too personal. Asking about his preferred sex positions or whether he's a tits or ass man could be overly arousing and put your boundaries in jeopardy. Similarly, questioning him about his most shameful regret or the pressures he might feel about his substantial hair loss could offend and threaten his personal boundaries.

THE BENEFITS PACKAGE

Having practiced this technique extensively, we have found that just about any guy will catch on and enjoy it. Instead of the first encounter being an awkwardly obvious hit-on situation, it becomes a loose and friendly interaction that spawns a genuine connection. We've also found that once the dude opens up, he becomes increasingly invested in keeping your attention because of how energized he feels in having an animated, challenging, and stimulating conversation with such a totally rad lady!

A quirky question is a brilliant way to show your true colors from the start. So the next time you spot a certain gent shining brighter than the rest, rouse your playful inner child and ask, "Have you ever seen aurora borealis?" As the splendorous sweetness of your question dawns on him, he'll know that swirls of purple in an Arctic sky could never compare to the force of nature standing right in front of him. And for that, he'll be thanking his lucky stars.

UNINHIBITED ENTHUSIASM

In the midst of enjoying your delicious tartar, you exclaim,
"I'm so enjoying this delicious tartar!"

Throw up your hands and say, "Yea-ah! Yea-ah!" Crank your life-lovin' volume up to high and let your inner excitement surge! Your uninhibited enthusiasm for the delights of life is *unbelievably attractive*. So don't hold back! When out with your fellow, give your joy the vociferous voice it deserves!

In this chapter we will explore why expressing your happiness without reservation is an insanely critical aspect of flirtation mastery. Your joy is the purest expression of your authenticity and is therefore one of the most potent points of attraction. So during the first encounter, we encourage you to pop the cork on your bottled-up delight and let the bursting bubbly flow! You will be stunned by how quickly you render him wholly intoxicated.

Uninhibited enthusiasm is the pinnacle of magnetism. Men are helplessly drawn in by expressions of glee simply because *they feel so good.* The power of the pleasure principle is not to be underestimated; humans are instinctively drawn to sources of thrill and excitement. When you allow yourself to be filled with unrestrained felicity, others will be vying for a front-row seat at your party. An exclamation like "That budding blue crocus might-ily pushing its way out of the mud is so beautiful, I can't stand it!" would thaw the heart of even the most die-hard cynic. An all-out enactment of a bombastic dance move would bring even the stodgiest stiff to life. A couple moments of belly-shaking laughter would crack the surface of even the chilliest chump. And letting out an uncivilized squeal in anticipation of your double-fudge brownie dessert would have any guy head over heels for you within seconds. You get the idea—so effervesce to your heart's content!

EXPRESS YOURSELF

This technique is especially provocative if he's the one providing the pleasure. *Nothing* pleases a man more than knowing he is pleasing you. They love to feel they chose a restaurant to your liking, suggested an especially delicious drink, or picked a movie you thoroughly enjoyed. So let him know what a spectacular job he's done. Unbridled appreciation is a powerful aphrodisiac whether it's in the bar, the brasserie, or the bedroom. What's more satisfying than knowing you have satisfied?

Our *bonne amie* Olivia tested the power of this theory one evening by letting the delight of her taste buds run away with her. Dig it:

Upon first meeting, Olivia and Ernest quickly established their mutual love for the oyster. He happened to grow up in Wellfleet on Cape Cod, which is famous for farming some of the tastiest mollusks on the East Coast—and of course he knew the best spot in New York City to find them. So on their first official date, they were off to a downtown seafood joint to enjoy the finest fruits of the sea. As Ernest squeezed lemon over a tray of twelve beauties, Olivia was already wild with excitement. She slurped the first into her mouth, and what happened next, she just couldn't help, "With my eyes closed, my shoulders did a little shake, and my hands and fingers shimmied up my body, over my head, and back down to finally rest on the table. I was ready for my next mouthful as

I exclaimed, 'These are *unbelievable!* Another, please!'" Naturally, Ernest was smiling and laughing—helplessly infected by her pleasure. There was no greater confirmation of an oyster-supplying job well done than Olivia's involuntary jig of joy. He certainly knew she was truly enjoying herself in his presence. And why not? The food was amazing, the company was fantastic, and she felt simply smashing. Sharing her feelings only intensified them, and by the time those twelve shells were empty, Ernest was happily hooked, marveling at what a fine catch he had sitting there across the way.

COOL AS A CUCUMBER?
SAVE IT FOR YOUR SALAD

We are flummoxed as to how "playing it cool" became the standard for anything, especially in *romance,* where the whole point is *passion.* So many people make the mistake of falling into this frosty trap, cutting themselves off from fully experiencing their natural excitement and enjoyment. Let's get real—it's not that fun to play unaffected. We've tried it. It was called seventh grade. And it kinda sucked. The whole unrelenting self-consciousness, where eye-rolling and disinterest in all things was mandatory if we wanted to avoid judgment from our peers, was actually just really boring. Those years might be long gone, but still it seems that so many of us are stuck in our insecure preteen postures.

The truth is that underneath the cool façade is fear: fear of opening up for fear of being attacked or hurt. There is a certain vulnerability that comes with expressing joy because it signifies a personal investment. When we really *care,* we run the risk of being disheartened or disappointed. There's the chance that someone will take the opportunity to dash our pure enthusiasm by saying, "Actually, your Barbie doesn't look great with that haircut." Or

"Huh . . . your sand castle is lopsided." Or "Santa Claus? Doesn't exist." We've all had experiences that made us vow never to put ourselves on the line again and to guard our hearts under the thickest shield of armadillo armor we can find. It's scary to really care after our hearts have been stomped, crushed, and ground into pulpy puree on a dirty sidewalk a couple of times. The letdown does quite a number on the ol' self-confidence.

But this is precisely why your uninhibited expressions of joy are so sexy! They convey your fearlessness, your lack of self-consciousness, your open heart, and your ability to blast open your true self. A simple exclamation like "Holy Tallulah, I LOVE this song! It's got the best syncopated harmonic structure I've ever heard! Listen!" shows that you are not afraid to take a risk and open yourself to passion and excitement. It would be easy to stay hidden under that armadillo armor forever, but life's true thrills happen when we are safe in our own soft skin, unconcerned with

SHERPA FLASH

A word of warning: Do not enact enthusiasm where there is none. Insincerity is never a good move, and any man worth his salt will see right through you. This technique is about giving yourself the freedom to completely experience your happiness and then letting it be expressed. It's not about faking it for effect. If you have trouble summoning genuine enthusiasm, recall your Joy List. Lead your date to the toy store that makes you giggle, sit with him by the river that fills your heart with bliss, take him for a scoop of the kona nut ice cream you can't seem to get enough of. Do the activities, eat the foods, visit the places that trigger true enthusiasm. Faking this technique will be immediately obvious and incredibly unsexy. And one last word of warning: Never, ever agree that you love something just because he does. If he has a passion for deep-sea fishing and you can't even stomach a night in a water bed, do not claim you share his passion! Next thing you know he'll be chartering a pontoon, packing the bait, and you'll be puking in your mouth. Not awesome.

the threat of attack from others and unbullied by the status quo. This is *true* self-assurance and confidence—qualities that are quite rare and therefore so very attractive. Add on a gush of pure, sparkly joy and you've got yourself a tantalizing cocktail concoction even Bill W. and Dr. Bob would be powerless against.

"WOW, YOU REALLY LIGHT UP THE ROOM!"

Enthusiasm is a highly infectious state of being. Your unself-conscious expressions of joy will saturate you with a radiant glow, infusing the whole room with a sense of lightness and freedom. Enthusiasm taps into the childlike innocence and wonder that most people yearn to regain. By standing, without reservation, in your excitement, you demonstrate that there is nothing to fear—you've shed your armadillo shield and you are still alive. Even better, you're really *living*. Your courage allows everyone to do the same, and nothing feels better than tearing off layers of mineralized exoskeleton after years of lugging around such a burden.

Our friend Leigh gives an extraordinary example of the power of enthusiasm to besot any gentleman. Take note:

Leigh does not take the future of our planet lightly. Neither does she have any interest in avoiding her part in saving the human race. So once she discovered the value of her own blood, she became very excited that she could give it, a pint at a time, every fifty-six days to help those in need. Pretty soon into her bloodletting habit Leigh met a young man by the name of Galen at a local Earth Day parade. He was an outdoorsy sort with a propensity for rock climbing and kayaking, and as they strolled through the crowd, chatting over the thrills of nature, Leigh was struck with a brilliant idea. "Hey! Do you want to give blood with me?" she asked. "Pardon?" he replied. "Have you ever given blood? Oh my God, it's so important! So many people are helped by it. You just go in there, and they hook this tube up to your arm and suck a pint of blood into this bag—for people who need transfusions! The Red Cross is just a block away." Galen, although unnerved by the proposition, simply couldn't resist her giddiness, so he dutifully followed her straight to the blood bank. As they lay in the recovery room an hour later, eating crackers and sipping apple juice, Leigh was glowing with joy because not only had she given a pint of blood that day, but Galen had given one too. "I couldn't help it—even though I was dizzy, I hopped out of my seat and hugged him spontaneously. He was still a little groggy, but he gave me the biggest smile and said, 'Should we consider this our first date?'" And so it was, the first of many.

SHERPA FLASH

If you're ever in the midst of an unabashedly enthusiastic exclamation and your guy gives you a sarcastic look or says something like "Whoa, calm down," or "Okay. Excited much?" this is your cue to drop him like a scorching hot potato. It is just not worth continuing on with a man who doesn't completely appreciate your heartfelt joy. This kind of sardonic behavior points to his own insecurity, cowardice, self-consciousness, and lack of gusto. Being passionate about different things is fine; he doesn't have to share in your excitement for beeswax glitter candles. But if he tries in any way to snuff out your zealous flame, you know it's time to smoke his ass straight out the door.

Sometimes enthusiasm emerges effortlessly, and other times it needs the right conditions to bloom. Referencing your Joy List is a phenomenal way to home in on environments that help your enthusiasm naturally thrive. Suggesting a particular place, cuisine, or activity that you know gets your passion pumping will set up the encounter or date for success. So if you're a complete plant fiend, suggest a sojourn to your favorite plant-filled atrium, and introduce him to the colors, textures, and smells contained in the acres of exotic greenery. Then just see if he can resist you after being in the presence of such an abundance of *aliveness.*

Enthusiasm is intoxicating. You've done the work to recognize what brings you joy, so don't hesitate to set yourself up for exciting experiences. There is nothing more interesting than a woman who is wholly *interested.*

PUNCH-DRUNK LOVE

This technique also gives your guy a taste of what it would feel like to be loved by you. He's thinking, "If she gets this excited about a gumball, imagine her excitement over a loving partner! And that guy could be me!" What man doesn't want that kind of frothily undivided attention? What man doesn't want you to get ecstatic over his bodily scent, his homemade stromboli, or about his choice in wallpaper? Show him you're not afraid to love what you love and he will do whatever it takes to be the object of your affections.

Your energetic conviction for the wonders, the mysteries, the pleasures, and even the pains of life is beyond beguiling. While you are riffing on the beauty of the moonlight's silvery glow, he'll be riveted by how beautiful you are in the glow of your own passion. If you remember anything, remember this maxim: To be supremely *interesting,* be supremely *interested.*

So when out on the town, if something really tickles you pink, don't try to hide the flush rising in your cheeks. Allow your enthusiasm to fill your entire being, spill over, and drench the night with unabashed jubilance. Do this and you'll leave your man dying to drown in your flood over and over again.

REVEALING INTELLIGENCE

*He brings up the latest political scandal; you make an astute
comparison to Nixon's downfall over Watergate*

They say there's nothing sexier than a woman with brains—
they're absolutely right. During the first encounter, please don't
hesitate to be the brightest bulb in the box. Take every opportunity to reveal the full scope of your intelligence!

Throughout this chapter, we'll explore how irresistible your
intellectual engagement can be and why prioritizing your intelligence creates unshakable confidence. So from here on out, we
encourage you to bypass the more common chatting choices,
pump up your brainpower, and let the fellow know you've got way
more on your mind than the weather.

Demonstrating the full scope of your particular intelligence
is one of the most important aspects of practicing successful
flirtation. Dropping a little-known fact about the Hundred Years
War would get anyone's ears perked. Reciting a bit of T. S. Eliot,
mentioning Martha Graham, or referencing a touch of Tibetan
theology are fabulous ways to ignite some *Smitten*esque sparks.
So if you happen to know a little something about the mating
rituals of the Pacific banana slug, let your wisdom flow. Revealing
the depth of your intelligence is deeply sexy, and he will surely
become completely enraptured as he watches your mouth form
some slippery five-syllable words: *Lasciviously, fiduciary, xenophobia,
hippopotamus, psychotherapy . . .*

THE EXPERT

Expertise (even almost-expertise, semi-expertise, or budding expertise) is undeniably attractive. Everyone admires the expert. Whether the subject is basket weaving in the pre-Columbian era or the best salons for hair weaving on Columbus Avenue, it doesn't matter. Knowing something about anything is universally appealing. Think of Mona Lisa Vito in *My Cousin Vinny*. So lovable and sexy to begin with, but dude, how much hotter was she after her expert automobile testimony on the witness stand?

Our human bodies are plainly three-dimensional; limited by their physical form. Basically, what you see is what you get. But our minds are so entirely unlimited! They are unrestrained by dimension, space, and time. The vastness and possibility of the engaged mind is utterly intoxicating. This free and boundless energy is what will draw men to you. Letting men catch a glimpse of your deep well of knowledge or showing them a touch of that cosmic female wisdom will create instant enchantment. Not because you have cast a spell, but because the limitlessness of what you offer is so exciting! It keeps them at the edge of their seats, always wanting more, always wanting to know what's going to come out of your mouth next. Revealing your expertise will make you so much more enticing. Just like Ms. Vito, it will totally rev your hotness way into the red.

A friend of ours, Caroline, recently experienced the luring effects of her expertise. Observe:

Caroline is a museum studies major with a particular interest in war memorialization. Yet she's hesitant to discuss such matters in social situations, afraid she might be labeled a Debbie Downer. Caroline isn't usually the one who dominates the spotlight in a group setting. She's a conservative, hometown kind of gal with wholesome good looks. She's not flashy—more pearl earrings than rhinestone hoops. Like sharks, men are often drawn to shiny, glittery objects, and as Caroline has noticed on many occasions, the flashier fish around her usually get the first bites. But on one particular night out, the subject of Vietnam came up in a discussion among the males. Someone kept reaching for the name of the carpet-bombing mission started by Johnson in '65. Caroline, being an expert on the subject, immediately chimed in. "I believe you are referring to Operation Rolling Thunder . . ." and the little sharkies started swarming. "I couldn't believe it. As I entered the conversation, they all circled around me, asking how I knew so much. It was like they were totally mesmerized by my knowledge of Vietnam, which I had always assumed was boring to everyone else. Suddenly, I was the center of attention for, like, the whole night." Caroline went home that evening with a few love bites in some unexpected places.

THE BIMBO FALLACY

If you recall, every *Smitten* flirtation technique requires one small thing—full and free expression of *who you truly are.* Your awesome intelligence is a powerful aspect of *who you truly are,* and as we just saw in the Caroline example, it is also highly attractive to men. Yet many women retain a fear of flexing their brain muscles during the first encounter. It's as if there is a chip wedged somewhere in the female social programming that reads *Smartypants are NOT, and will NEVER be, sexy—but Daisy Dukes are!*

Why do women still have this idea that men are most often attracted to the prototype airheaded bimbo, and that a woman with intellect is sure to be a bore? We repeatedly *still* hear women say that they believe revealing how smart, knowledgeable, or clever they are will intimidate men and scare them off. Many other women won't admit to diluting their smarts, but their behavior still reflects this antiquated belief.

Take a peek into any one of your past or present relationships and observe your own behavior. Notice where you might subtly subscribe to the idea that being a passive airhead will reap more male attention. Ever catch yourself saying, "I don't know" when you really do? Ever keep quiet for fear he'll criticize your ideas? You might also root around for any stale bimbos-are-better beliefs. What did Mom do when politics came up at a dinner party—check the casserole? What did Dad do if Mom got passionate about politics at the dinner party—tell her to check the casserole?

One prime example is a young Nebraskan-born friend of ours who happens to be bombshell-beautiful *and* smart as a whip. One would think she would be eager to show off the entire package of who she truly is. But instead, this bright young babe actually adopted a bogus Valley Girl–type of voice in order to mask her awesome intellect, believing she would not be attractive to men if they knew she had such a gifted mind. We are entirely dumbfounded by this idea!

First, if a man really is intimidated by your intelligence, it's because he is insecure about his own. If then, out of his own insecurity, he labels your braininess unattractive, *he is not a man worthy of your presence.* Period. Second, when you assume that a man will be turned off by your smarts, you shortchange him and yourself. Believing that a woman's strong intellect is a turnoff is the totally inane attitude of an immature jerk. So if you jump to the conclusion that he will be turned off by your brain, you instantly label him an inane, immature jerk. He might turn out to be that way, but you could at least give him a chance to prove you wrong first. Third, if you play dumb for men, you will attract dumb men, which is probably not your intention.

You see, this is the thing: You *must* set a standard for yourself. When you honestly put forth your smarts, you set the bar for what you want and expect in your personal interactions. This is true for a simple exchange, a night of conversation, or a long-term partnership. Truthfully representing the capacity of your mind means you are honoring yourself. This is of utmost importance. Freely expressing your intelligence is a way of loving yourself, but it also happens to make men love you too. It garners immediate respect—makes the man sit up, listen, and fully engage. It dissolves all social boundaries. He could be the latest hotshot celebrity or the puffed-up heir to some European business empire; it doesn't matter. Your wit can cut through all perceived societal barriers and keep *any* guy on his toes. We've been there. We know this. It just works.

THE QUERIST

In the course of attracting interesting and intelligent men, it's inevitable that you will come across gentlemen who introduce ideas and topics you know nothing about. So if you find yourself in the dark, instead of shutting down, use these situations as opportunities to shine even brighter . . . by switching on your curiosity.

For example, let's say your theater buff friend has dragged you to the opening night of *A Doll's House,* and during intermission you find yourself waiting in the candy line, wondering why the miniatures haven't yet made it onstage. Suddenly, a gorgeous gentleman behind you asks what you think the father of modern realism would say about this new production of his classic. You're thinking, *The father of what?* Seeing as this is your first play since *Cats* at the Winter Garden Theater, you have absolutely no idea what he's talking about. At this point, instead of nodding and muttering something vague because you feel ashamed for not knowing more about the arts, just ask! Not knowing does not mean you're dumb; it just means you don't know *yet*. You don't need to feel stupid or embarrassed if you're clueless. Intelligence is also revealed in your curiosity and eagerness to ask questions that extend beyond your areas of expertise. By choosing to ask, you allow a whole world of inspired learning and sizzling dialogue to open up.

So you might say, "Who's the father of what? I haven't seen a play since I was twelve." He might answer, "Oh, Ibsen, the playwright. He basically changed the whole style of drama and influenced every writer that came after him." Cool, you learned something new. Now you can pursue numerous avenues of conversation stemming from this initial exchange. Maybe you'll be inspired to share some thoughts on your favorite writer, articulate your preference for film, or relay your Broadway-induced ailurophobia.

This state of open-minded curiosity is just where you want to be. He'll pick up on the excitement you exude as you explore unknown territory. Your willingness to still enjoy yourself while beyond your comfort zone is incredibly attractive. It's another expression of that free and boundless energy that men are so drawn to. If you had instead opted for closing yourself off because of your theatrical ignorance, then the whole cycle of fun flirtation would have never even started. So take our advice: Ask when you don't know. You'll crack open infinite *Smitten* possibilities. It wasn't curiosity that killed the cat; apathy is the more likely suspect. Poor little kitty. *Let her memory live again!*

Of course when freely exchanging ideas, it's natural to disagree on certain issues. But often when getting to know someone, conflict can feel like a big no-no. The fear of awkwardness tends to keep us on the *via media.* You might feel it's more appealing to act agreeable, but we have consistently found that truthfully speaking your mind during conflict will actually make you much *more* desirable. So if you disagree, say it. Having the pluck to stand by what you believe is super-friggin' sexy. It shows courage, confidence, and strength of character. What are you gonna do, cram yourself into a nice little box of yes's just so he'll like you? No way, man, *free expression* is the name of this game. He's gonna like you because you're ballsy and free, not because you're a gutless yellow belly.

SHERPA FLASH

One thing to keep in mind during brainier exchanges is that nobody likes a snob. We are certainly not encouraging you to list the main points of your Harvard graduate thesis with a smug air. Brash statements of intellectual superiority are the foulest of turnoffs because they end up squashing rather than enticing a connection. The most alluring intellectual communicates her understanding of a given subject in a way that includes the man and encourages open and amusing conversation.

Men enjoy a little challenge; it's in their nature. So if you think his view on the future of industrial farming stinks, tell him so— but always with good-humored spirit. Conflict doesn't mean we want you to engage in an all-out punching match. Ouch. We're talking about little playful love taps. Like baby cheetahs exchanging tiny swats with their paws but never exposing the sharp claws underneath. You don't need to draw blood in order to speak the truth of your mind. Besides, his focus would then be on his bloody wounds and off your bloody good point.

STOKING THE FIRE

If you want a partner who is passionate and smart, you must express your passion and smarts. Unfortunately, after our formal schooling, we settle into our chosen professions and intellectual growth and discovery tend to wane. A couple hours of mindless TV every night easily becomes the after-work habit. Cool weekend workshops are bypassed for the same old shopping routine. Reading is regulated to gossip magazines loaded with celebrity drama and weight-loss tips. But beware! Too much of this fluffy stuff will extinguish the fire of passion that burns in your brain! It is precisely this brainy passion that we urge you to continue to cultivate. Its energy fuels your innate magnetism, allure, and charm. It is an age-old truth that to be interesting, you must be interested. So allow yourself to delve fully into your hottest curiosity, whether it be the formation of Volcaniclastic rock, the myth of Pele, or the Maunder Minimum. *Go forth and stoke the fire of your mind.*

If you don't know what you love, or you feel cut off from what you're passionate about, explore! Recall your favorite childhood activities and see where they lead you. Pop into a bookstore, grab the first book you're instinctively drawn to, and see what happens. Rent a documentary you've never heard of, see a play you know nothing about, or visit a little-known gallery just because. Get hungry. Get curious. Open yourself to the wonderment of life. When we stop growing and expanding, we die. Don't die.

There are certain social experiences, however, that are so anxiety-provoking that you may actually *want* to die. Like being the silent one in the circle, wracking your brain for something to add or second-guessing anything you might like to say. Then feeling so out of place that you spend much of the evening picking lint off your skirt in order to appear occupied. But by allowing your intellect to emerge, you'll always have something interesting to bring to the table. Having the self-assurance that you can participate in any conversation allows you to relax and enjoy yourself. When you're in this state of ease, you are in a state of confidence. This kind of intellectual confidence is unfailing and unquestionable. It is the confidence that you have a wide array of unique thoughts and ideas that will enable you to be fearlessly engaged no matter what the situation. It is the confidence that your contributions will be met with respect and appreciation. It is the confidence that you can even sit comfortably by yourself, entertained by your own fascinating mind without needing the attention or approval of others. This relaxed self-assurance is and will always be the zenith of sexiness.

Therefore when you're out on the town chatting it up with a fellow, don't hesitate to reveal the full scope of your intelligence. And if you must talk about the weather, don't just comment on how frizzy the rain makes your hair. Use the precipitation as an opportunity to discuss the wonders of the hydraulic cycle as you recount your virga experience in the Mojave. By embracing this brainy technique, it's certain that you will leave him 100 percent thunderstruck.

PURELY PINK

*You order the raspberry soufflé and absentmindedly
trace hearts in the crème anglaise*

You needn't be born of sea foam or prompt flowers to bloom at
your feet as you stroll toward Cyprus to successfully embody this
entrancing technique. Your own distinctive brand of womanli-
ness is more than sufficient. In this chapter, we will explore how
releasing just a touch of your unique femininity will have your
Adonis worshipping at your holy temple of awesomeness for all
of eternity. So unbind your streak of purely female energy and let
your X chromosome swell during the first encounter or date!

Aphrodite had her fanciful style, just as each of us ladies has
our own natural way of expressing our femininity. This creative
force rises from deep within, superceding the mere fact of our
physical sex and manifesting itself in an assortment of ways. It
may arise as girliness: a Lolita who adores strawberry shortcake
and white ruffled skirts. It may emerge as an earth mother: the
nurturing, organic, natural-as-milk-and-honey brand of babe.
It could materialize like a minx: sleek, black, and undeniably in
charge. Or maybe it manifests more like a mermaid: forlorn and
shimmery, with a salty, sun-bleached mane and a far-off gaze. We
are not instructing you to dress up in cat ears or a fishtail; we are
simply saying get in touch with how you naturally experience your

inner goddess and then allow those rays to shine. A girly giggle, an ecstatic moment with a blooming bromeliad, a slight purr at the sight of your filet, or a few hair twirls around your beach-bronzed fingers will easily send your sailor overboard with adulation.

SIGN OF THE TIMES

Femininity has a long and weary history fraught with exploitation, demonization, and rampant misinterpretation. It has been overplayed and underplayed, attacked and revered, suppressed and hyperexpressed. It has been used to gain advantage and dismissed to simulate equality. The mere mention of the word "feminist" makes most of us feel as though we are suddenly on eggshells— tiptoeing along, hoping not to offend and get burned at the stake.

Our perspective of ourselves as women often gets distorted through our gender politics paranoia. In certain situations we overact, playing up a picture of dumb helplessness, morphing into the cartoonish rendition of a weak, tearful, bubblegum-blowing, wide-eyed, vacant girl. Other times we swing to the opposite end of the scale and become an angry, man-hating, lipstick-scoffing, power-hungry woman. We probably haven't come to many solid conclusions on the definition of femininity because how can we adequately pin it down? Should we purposely embrace our female qualities or try to shed them? Is it nature or nurture that causes us to crave the finest facial products and the softest taffeta party wear? Why can't we get past the whole issue and just *be*?

Whatever your connotations of the word or the concept, for our purposes in this chapter, we'd like to help you understand your femininity to be divine, exquisite, and compelling. It is not something to manipulate or hide, but rather to celebrate and explore. Instead of being swayed by popular opinion about the normal ways to think and act as a female, endeavor to make your own discoveries about your womanhood. "No, I'm not a peach; I'd say I'm more of a persimmon." "Don't really feel that connected to Venus—I think I'm actually a Jupiter kind of lady." "Never went for kitten heels myself; always preferred a solid pair of clogs instead." There is never a right or a wrong way for you to express your femaleness. Whatever part of the spectrum you fall on, however you desire to put forth your yin—it's heavenly, as long as it is *your choice.* Undoubtedly, if there's one thing that has been sorely lacking in the history of womankind, it's been our power and privilege to choose. So muster up your newly minted free will and exercise that choice in all aspects of life—the expression of your muliebrity included.

OPPOSITES ATTRACT

Even on the worst of the worst days, you've always got one sure thing going for you when it comes to attracting men: You are a woman. You are different from them. Allowing your pinkness to trickle through will only add to this tempting dissimilarity. Doing things that men simply can't do or just wouldn't ever think of doing is forever surprisingly sexy.

Let's have a look at this technique in action in the following example from Simone:

One evening after a summer painting class, Duke, a fellow student, asked Simone if she would like to join him for a bite at the café around the corner. Having had a secret crush on him since day one, Simone readily agreed. As the night progressed, they happily chatted through chicken fingers and then moved on to tea and dessert. As Duke's eyes dropped to peruse the extensive menu of sweets, Simone developed a sudden fascination with the tiny vat of honey that accompanied her chamomile. It glistened and gleamed, it oozed and shined. *How funny!* she thought. *It looks just like my new sparkly nude lip gloss.* So on her pout it went. When Duke looked up, she puckered her lips and asked, "Does this look like lip gloss?" Duke stuttered, "U-Uh, yes. Y-Yes, it does. What is it?" "Honey!" Simone replied. At which point, his jaw fell off. "Oh. Well, it, uh, looks really nice. Uh, it looks good on you." It wasn't until that moment that Simone realized the implications of her honey-smearing ways. She had been so engrossed in the girly pleasure of discovering a new method of turning food into beauty product (blueberry juice stain for the cheeks, mayonnaise for moisture-thirsty locks) that she didn't realize the greater effect she had produced. Her feminine creativity conveyed complex provocative allusions that had caught her unawares. It was clear to see that Duke was done for. "It's true—one look at my *glacé de meil* and he was toast." Nobody had any doubt about who his queen bee was the following week in class.

Your feminine mystique is more than lacy lingerie, curvy hips, or the simple fact that you have breasts. It is your whole entire womanly package—your creativity, resourcefulness, deep optimism, sage wisdom, and playfulness! You see, men don't think of turning honey into lip balm. They rarely even use lip balm. They don't see twelve solutions to every problem. They see three. They don't think to press flowers between the pages of a dictionary or understand the vital importance of sharing a bathroom stall with their best friend. Our instinctual differences are what make us unique, and ultimately so damn appealing to each other. The essence of your yin energy is a highly potent elixir. Let leak just one tiny droplet of your siren song of femininity and you are likely to find him crashing hard onto your cliffs with unadulterated attraction.

SHERPA FLASH

As with all the other flirtation techniques, this method does not do well under pressure. Anything forced or contrived will indubitably fall flat. Honey on the lips for the sake of coming off sexy will only come off as artificial. The goal is all-natural. Think organic. Meditate on whatever images of femininity you are drawn to and notice how they arise in you. Then when an action, a movement, an outfit, a dance, or a giggle starts to bubble up, let it. This technique is about expressing that female energy when it genuinely wants to emerge, not forcing it for a predetermined effect.

NURTURE YOUR FEMININITY

There is no energy on the planet more powerful than that of the feminine. The essence of femininity is pure creation. Ancient civilizations honored Mother Earth above all. They believed it was she who had birthed the rivers, sprouted the trees, built the mountains, dug the valleys, turned the tides, and reared all the creatures and critters on the planet. As women, we possess the ultimate power of creation—we give life! We grow babies in our bellies, using our own bodies to supply the blood and nutrients that will turn a microscopic seed into a fully realized being. Female energy is regenerative and rejuvenating. It is the primal, vital force that runs throughout the Earth, the oceans, the plants, and the stars. It is the life that courses through our very own veins.

By recognizing and cultivating this fundamental force within you, you honor your own essential nature. But you need not ever birth a child to develop your feminine puissance; there are all sorts of ways to nurture your womanly essence. In fact, chances are you already do. It is present when you chop basil and cook a meal for your friends, sustaining their bodies and souls. It is there when you dig a hole in the soil and plant petunias in anticipation of summer. It is with you when you brush paint across a canvas, string pink pearls along a strand, strum your guitar, water your ferns, present a speech, write a short story, film a movie, sing onstage, weave a rug, sculpt a vase, or design your dream home. Every time you create, you nurture the almighty feminine.

So envelop yourself in these creative expressions as a way to cherish and celebrate what it means to be a woman on the planet. By making time to prune your peonies or knit your own mittens, you will become more familiar with your uniquely divine feminine essence. Conscious acts of creation not only pay tribute to the ancient lineage of females who came before, but they also enhance the glow of your own irresistible fecundity.

BOYS MUST BE BOYS

In the precious moments when your goddessness is set free, you provide a rare opportunity for the fellow in your presence. You allow him the space to embody his own inner god—to be a man. In this day and age, that is an uncommon liberty. Not only have women become bewildered by the touchy terrain of social equality, so have men. Often they do not know which messages to adhere to—to open the door or not open the door, to make a move or keep his hands in his pockets, to take the check or go Dutch. Some don't want to make the wrong move and offend, but many, unfortunately, haven't even learned the ways of a proper gentleman. Not that we want to regress to some antiquated era of male dominance, but it is nice to be offered a seat on the subway, taken to lunch on occasion, and in general be treated like the ladies we are. Of course, this is while still retaining the option to refuse as well as the resources to provide for ourselves.

Even if some guys today don't know the first thing about good manners, they still contain that intrinsic desire to be the man. Deep down, all men want to be an argonaut—a hero of humanity traveling the high seas in search of a bundle of golden sheep's hair. It's encoded in their DNA. By letting them have their moments of manly man glory, you provide them with an exceptional gift. They might not recognize it on a conscious level—most men don't get around to examining their Herculean heroic yearnings—but they will feel it, even if just for a moment, on a visceral level. They'll venture home feeling strong, proud, and able. They won't need to know the deeper reasons for their broadened chest and raised chin; they will just know that they can hardly wait to take that glorious girl (you) out again!

A little tale from the lovely Leda:

Leda was out with a new guy one evening, and after a delight-ful little dinner he insisted on walking her home, which was per-fectly sweet. Their route led them through Washington Square Park, and as they strolled by one of those artfully overfilled garbage cans, a huge rat scuttled past their feet—almost close enough to take a nibble off Leda's bare toes! She instinctively shrieked and grabbed her date's muscled forearm. "Now, I grew up in the real country. I'm very used to mice, snakes, and all sorts of creepy crawlers sharing my home. But a Washington Square rat crossing my path . . . ugh. I couldn't help but yelp!" The point is, the appearance of the rat had an upside. "My guy thought my near heart attack was the cutest thing ever." Leda had shown her fully self-sufficient I-don't-rely-on-anyone side all through dinner. Then when her pink underbelly showed, her guy was so pleasantly taken aback, he offered to give her a piggyback ride the rest of the way! "Weird, I know! I normally would never accept, thinking, *What if I'm too heavy, or what if he gets tired,* but it was only two more blocks to my apartment and he obviously worked out, so I figured I could let him be my hero for the next four minutes." Leda hopped on, and they laughed and laughed the whole way home. When he dropped her off at her graffitied front stoop, he wore the adorable glow of a job well done. It was absolutely one of Leda's best dates ever.

Obviously, our friend could have made it home safely on her own two feet, but she took the opportunity to have a little fun with her maidenliness. Just as it's sexy for us to behave in ways that men don't, the reverse is also true. It's unlikely that we would offer to literally carry our dates home on our backs (we ladies do this emotionally for our men all the time, but that's a different book altogether), so when he's vying to flex his manly muscles, let him. Because you don't actually need to be saved, you can comfortably play Helen to his Menelaus. As long as you are both choosing the roles, this type of horsing around can be an absolute aphrodisiac.

So, darling nubile nymph, allow your femininity to bud, bloom, and blossom! Revel in the fragrance of your completely original scent. Bathe in the brilliance of your own divine essence. With your purely pink glow on high, the only quandary you're likely to encounter is choosing from all the plentiful fish in the Aegean.

SECRET THOUGHTS

Before your dirty martini even arrives, you let slip some secret thoughts

Like it or not, you, my dear, are a very strange specimen. Sure, you act nice and normal on the outside, but you've got a surreal internal world that's positively brimming with the oddest inklings, the weirdest urges, and the most bizarre insights. You may have been warned to keep that fantastical freakishness to yourself, but this technique will show how glimpses of your idiosyncratic inner life are actually quite mesmerizing to your male counterparts. So embrace your penchant for the peculiar and allow those eccentric inspirations to rise up from the deepest folds of your fathomless psyche.

The next time a dude asks if you're digging your drink, try remarking, "The truth is, my love of dirty martinis actually stems from a fascination with what it would feel like to drown in the brackish waters of the Baltic Sea." Or perhaps if you two are crammed together on a packed patio, you could whisper, "Sometimes in a crowd like this, I like to imagine we're all one giant amoeba, searching for tasty bacteria to digest in our communal vacuole." Or if he's your study buddy, you could try, "Often when solving a trigonometry problem, I attempt to turn my brain inside out and catch a glimpse of what's really happening in there, but the process always seems to elude me." Then, of course, you could also say, "You know, Joseph Campbell's work really exacerbated my latent neurosis." Or "I'm fighting the strongest urge to lick the gooseberries on that wallpaper." Or "I had the best dream last night—I was gliding through a Jell-O pit in a lawn chair . . ."

What we're saying here is flaunt your Freudian slips, spill your Jungian slides, and let your esoteric self reign from its kooky, crooked throne! The idea is to crack open the channel between your unconscious stirrings and conscious communication, releasing bits and pieces of your simmering, mysterious self. This is about allowing those normally unspoken thoughts to cross the threshold from suppression into expression. When you do this, your illimitable uniqueness will transport the dynamic into another realm—where he'll be wholly haunted by the unexpected enigma in his midst.

YOU, UNCENSORED

There are an awful lot of unspoken codes of conduct that shape our world. Codes about how to dress, what to drive, how to behave, what to say, and, more importantly, how *not* to do all of those things. These are the blocks on which we have built our collective agreement of reality. They define what is normal. Through the presence of these codes, we all get a nice little illusion of control. We count on each other to not behave in ways that would puncture this picture ("The sky is falling!"). Human decency compels us to conform to certain boundaries and social norms, but alas, the whole system is really just a fantasy.

Reality is what we make it, and society is just a bunch of people agreeing on somewhat the same version of that reality. The social rules that govern us are arbitrary. We could have just as easily agreed to say hello to each other with an elbow rub rather than a handshake, or decided that lip plates are more provocative than earrings, or that it is incredibly rude to close the bathroom door while we relieve ourselves. We hold so tightly to these codes that we did not choose—to the point of letting them regularly stifle what we do, say, express, and reveal.

Of course, for civilization to function, we must suppress our instinctive sexual, libidinal, and homicidal urges and suffer our discontents. But there is so much more to each of us than what our proper social standards allow. There are dimensions within ourselves that are so unique, so inexplicable, that even Sigmund himself couldn't begin to interpret what they mean. No matter how many times you lie on that sofa, no one could ever get to the bottom of the wonderful world of you. Every tickle of insight, each inexplicable flash of imagery, every random revelation could be unspooled forever and ever, leading you farther down the rabbit hole of your own mind.

The point is, those very flashes, urges, and insights that you might never have considered fit for small talk are actually so scintillating, they can stimulate unknown spheres of communication and connection. There are bigger ideas, concepts, metaphors, and archetypal links embedded in our secret musings than what we generally show the world. When you share these insights, you glide past small talk and go right for big talk. A bigger truth resonates between him and you, and an understanding is struck at an uncommon level. By sharing your inner visions, you will meet at a mystical place that's far more profound than any amount of time you two could spend together horizontal on a leather couch.

For a man, getting a glimpse of your surreal inner life is like seeing a sleeve slip off your shoulder, briefly revealing your silky skin beneath. It's like catching a whiff of the nape of your neck, or brushing up against the curve of your hip. It's an intensely provocative sensation, creating a split second of unexpected intimacy that will leave him lucidly dreaming of more.

Let's look at how this atypical technique played out with our friend Brianne in a typical man-meeting environment . . . her stepsister's wedding:

In appearance, Brianne is a fairly modest lass. She stays with a palette of muted mauves and cornflower blues, and has never been the type to mess with black nail polish, diamond-studded thongs, or hot-magenta lipstick. But her pointy fairy ears and the mischievous curl of a smile hint at the peculiar world swirling just beneath the surface of her understated exterior. And on this particular afternoon, in the shade of a big white wedding tent in the New England countryside, a sweet young chap by the name of Robert had the occasion to behold some of the unusual stuff that Brianne is made of.

During the toasts, Robert and Brianne were seated side by side. The father of the bride was reading a quote that described the marital union as a symbolic melding of two into one. Brianne was rather put off by this idea, and leaned over to whisper into Robert's ear, "That sounds disgusting! Like how when people are bedridden, their skin starts to grow into the sheets."

"Now, I realize that was not the most appetizing image for a young lady to blurt out at a wedding ceremony," recalls Brianne, "but I had just read some news clipping about a large lady who had to be surgically removed from her bed linens, and I couldn't resist. Anyway, Robert apparently didn't mind. He became surgically attached to *me* the rest of the night. I mean, he barely left my side!" Upon making his exit, Robert slipped her his number with a note stating that anyone who would liken a biblical verse to skin grafting was someone he had to see again.

One fun way to use this technique is to make an unusual observation about the man you are speaking to. People love to hear about themselves. We love to know what others think of us, how they see us, what strikes them about our looks, our speech, our behavior. Maybe his twinkly eyes make him look like a wizard, or his demanding, presumptuous manner causes you to guess that he's an only child, or the way his temper flares up gives him the distinct air of a Scorpio. Instead of keeping those observations to yourself, share them. Don't be afraid to use your awesome powers of intuitive perception on the men you encounter. Even if your perception is not entirely flattering, it doesn't matter. He'll be so intrigued by your curious remarks that he won't be able to resist pursuing how and why you came to your astute conclusions.

SHERPA FLASH

As with every *Smitten* technique, it is never advisable to falsify anything. So please don't go plagiarizing Plath or stealing from Silverstein in your efforts to be abnormal (although you might find some rich inspiration there). This technique is about revealing slivers of your particular worldview. It will not work if you fake it. It will only work if it is a genuine observation, recollection, thought, or question that emanates from your authentic, eccentric experience.

THE GAINS

Revealing your secret thoughts conveys true confidence, the sexiest attribute in our worldly existence. The lady who will allow her most unusual musings to be heard by a stranger is someone who has a deep feeling of acceptance about who she is. It is ballsy, bold, and fearless. It displays an unusual reserve of personal power. It says "I am comfortable enough to allow myself to not only be

SHERPA FLASH

Fortunately, as you continue your process of self-realization, these images and insights will start to become more accessible. The work you are doing to gain an understanding of your feelings, thoughts, and behaviors—to fully accept yourself—has the effect of lessening psychic anxiety. Anxiety distracts us and blocks creative ideas from reaching our consciousness. But with this anxiety tempered by your newfound self-acceptance, you make space for your unconscious musings to surface. So all kidding aside, we must thank old Freud for starting up this therapeutic self-acceptance stuff. Without him, we would never have gotten the chance to examine our Oedipal/Electran urges to bed our fathers and kill our mothers. What a sobering thought.

conscious of my subconscious, but to defy social norms by expressing what I'm really thinking." Where most wouldn't dream of articulating any abnormality in themselves, the welcoming of your magical thoughts is part of what makes you so irresistible. Within this confidence is also the knowledge that even if the guy doesn't get it, all is well. You are assured enough to express yourself, and nobody's blank stares will shake your dedication to your truth, regardless of how irrational, perplexing, or queer it may seem.

Furthermore, by communicating from this unseen place, you give your guy permission to express the strange and unique essence of who *he* is. Most men are taught that they must be solid, stoic, and stable. They rarely get the invitation to be open, unusual, and free. He craves the opportunity to show you all of his dimensions, to put on his philosopher's cap and have a reason to take his dusty copy of *Discourse on Method* off the bookshelf once again. He will be flattered and thankful that in your presence, *all* of him is allowed—not just the clichés of manliness that social conditioning has bound him to in the past.

Like an orphic song, your secret thoughts have the power to transform the textures of everyday, ordinary reality and reveal hidden aspects of your truest self. So during your evenings out, don't hesitate to open that trap door and take him for a ride down the passageways of your subconscious. Your mind's cosmic musings will have him faithfully following you not only throughout this world, but past the threshold of time and space into the unknown dimensions of the mysterious beyond.

SHERPA FLASH

It can sometimes be difficult to discern which secret thoughts are appropriate to reveal. Should you dare say any old thing that's on your mind? Or should you only give away particular tidbits? With this technique, as a general rule it is best to reveal the thoughts that allow you to stay comfortable and safe, no matter what his reaction is. He might say, "Oh, that's awesome/gross/stupid/interesting/crazy . . ."—none of which should bother you. If you need him to have a positive response to make you feel secure, then don't reveal that thought. For example, say you're chatting with your guy and you realize his model looks or Ivy League education have you feeling quite intimidated. If you choose to reveal this and say, "You know, I'm feeling quite intimidated by you right now," and are needing him to feel equally awestruck by you, don't reveal that thought. He may not respond in kind, and you don't want to give him the power to make you feel unworthy or hurt with a response that isn't what you had hoped for. On the other hand, if he just told you he's a rocket scientist and you say, "Wow, I'm feeling kind of intimidated," that's different. In this case you are making a lighthearted statement, and his response really has no bearing on your sense of self. See the difference? Do not expose your wounds or insecurities if you need him to take care of them, or if he doesn't seem like the kind of guy who is sensitive enough to safely guard your heart's precious bits of information.

DECISIVE DECISIONS

With endless options for dinner downtown,
you declare exactly what strikes your fancy

Whoever said women are ill-equipped to make decisions ought to be prepared to bite their tongue! We ladies are not only extremely adept at decisiveness, we are also extraordinarily enticing while making a firm statement of desire. So don't shy away from knowing what you know—your certitude is the ticket that will take your charisma past the point of no return.

Throughout this chapter, we will explore why defying the stereotype of the wishy-washy woman during the first encounter or date is so unthinkably sexy. By uttering just one frank declaration of your particular preference, you are likely to stun him with your clarity of character. Pretty soon he'll be begging to trail your trolley all the way to the end of the line—or the ends of the Earth. Wherever you are, that's precisely where he'll want to be.

Apathy is an anti-aphrodisiac. There is no energy in "I don't know, I don't care, whatever." Acting wishy-washy is duller than dishwater. By offering no suggestions about what you long to feel, see, or do, you kill the momentum and flatten the fizz of romantic excitement. But declaring exactly what you want makes the moment buzz and demonstrates your mesmeric confidence. So if he is buying you a drink, state that you would like a Sazerac, extra lemon, and hold the bitters, please. If you have just left the restaurant, propose that you skip the cab and stroll through the park to breathe in the night's burgeoning honeysuckle. When choosing the flavor for your hookah, go ahead and order the rose you've been wondering about, even if the waiter suggests mint. Trust your desires and offer your vision to the unfolding evening. Even if your guy doesn't share the same urges, your inspiration will inspire the encounter to continually come to life.

HAZY FOCUS

Your preferences and cravings are reflections of who you truly are; they are vibrant conduits for your authenticity. Yet so many women are too timid to vocalize their wishes. We get shy, think it is more pleasing to acquiesce, or we worry we'll come across as being pushy or demanding if we speak up for our wants. When we women are faced with a decision during a date, it's often "Oh, I don't know what I'd like to eat . . . What sounds good to you?" Or "I'm not sure what I'd like to see. I heard that Spanish film is kind of good. What do you think?" Or "I don't know if you should come up—do you really want to?"

But most of the time we *do* know what we want to eat, we *do* know what we want to see, and we definitely know whether we want him to come up or not—because we know who we are. (What do you think all that work in Part One was about?) Refraining from speaking what you know is actually a feeble cop-out. If you are uncertain of yourself, he'll undoubtedly be uncertain of you. However, by clearly and openly making a decision, you convey real personal power, centered poise, and true confidence. Basically, you become crazy-frickin' sexy.

Your sudden sexiness will not be because you and your dude have the exact same urge. ("Oh my God! You want a slice of key lime pie right now too? We are totally soul mates!") It will come from the dynamism of your self-awareness. Your man will perk up and pay attention because he's finally discovered a woman who knows herself well enough to know what she wants, and is self-assured enough to express it. A gal who's not afraid to stand beneath a bare bulb and say, "This is who I am—like it or leave it, Buster!" That kind of confidence is a cornerstone of your temptress talents, whether or not meringue whets his palette on that particular evening.

Please see an example of superior decisive decision date work from our chum Carrie:

Carrie's reserved nature might at first make her seem like a lady who is hesitant to divulge her actual wants. Her tendency to mull things over as opposed to jumping right in with an opinion can make her seem less than self-assured. However, one May day as Carrie was approaching the finals for her master's in cinema studies, she was quite pleased when Timothy, a particularly cute fellow film geek, casually suggested they brush up on the French New Wave together. Carrie agreed, but she wasn't sure how to respond when he asked where she'd like to meet. After standing there in limbo for a few moments, Carrie resolved to bypass the obvious suggestions, such as the library or the student center, and instead cut right to the chase. "Meet me at two p.m. on the eighth floor of the music building. Bring a pillow to sit on. I'll show you my favorite study spot."

The following afternoon, Tim showed up at two on the dot on the eighth floor, cushion in hand. Carrie led him down a long hall to an old practice room that had been unused for years. As Tim made himself comfortable on the parquet, his eyes bulged at the mysterious room filled with aging musical instruments and was immediately transfixed by its cinematic appeal. Then his gaze quickly shifted to Carrie, and he proceeded to spend the lion's share of the afternoon going on about her striking mise-en-scène and wanting to know what other special spots she had discovered on campus. "It was like he suddenly really saw me for the first time. Honestly, I didn't know if he invited me to study because he liked me or just because he's sort of ADD and could have used the help. But I do know for sure that my decisiveness about where to meet brought his attention fully and completely onto me." Carrie's decisive study decision wasn't just a great opportunity to have a little private time with Tim; it provided him with a window into her existence. From that point on, Carrie was the one and only figure visible in Timothy's romantic viewfinder.

Clearly stating your desire, as Carrie did, begins to paint a picture of who you truly are in a very material sense. It brings into focus bits and pieces of your world. The more specific you are, the more his imagination will crackle and spark with curiosity. Your vision, especially if it is different from anything he would ever think of, will perplex and stimulate him. He will be compelled to offer more of himself and want to explore the nuances of your varying preferences. One of the happiest parts of partnership with another is the opportunity to experience the world they live in: the places they go to, cuisines they relish, and sights they love to see. By being up-front with your personal predilections, the encounter will quickly become a richer, more satisfying experience for both of you.

STAND AND BE COUNTED

Decisiveness doesn't just display your charming idiosyncrasies. It also communicates that you are your own authority, capable of making clear decisions to move your life forward. You are not Laura in *The Glass Menagerie,* passively dusting your animal figurines, forever waiting for a man to show up and lift you from your dreary, club-footed destiny. You are a vital, self-possessed woman who can take care of herself. This message is more influential than it may seem. If a man is going to jump on the relationship wagon with you, he's got to know if you can harness a horse and align an axle, should push come to shove.

Believe it or not, simply stating that you would like a glass of the 2007 Pinot Noir and the lamb, rare, with a side of turnips rather than green beans will communicate to your dude that he can count on you to act if you are ever stuck in the middle of a bayou with wagon wheels sinking and Clydesdales starting to revolt. Decisiveness is next to godliness. One too many floundering moves and you've just spelled the difference between a long, healthy life together and death by swamp-logged lungs.

SHERPA FLASH

"I want a golden egg NOW, Daddy."
There is a vast divide between decisiveness and brattiness. Knowing what you want does not mean you must always *get* what you want. This technique is not about controlling the situation so everything goes your way. We are not suggesting you whine, sulk, and stomp your foot because you've been dreaming about peaches all evening and the table next to you just got the very last cobbler. This method is really about communicating your preferences without shame or insecurity while still maintaining your grace and dignity—a rare combination in women, especially young women. Embodying this kind of inner power will hastily garner interest and admiration from all those in your presence.

This technique relates to Chapter Two, in the eradication of your victim mentality. Your ability to be decisive is directly linked to your awareness that you are not, in the slightest, a damsel in distress in need of some sword-swinging prince to order your Caesar for you. Practicing decisiveness is practicing assertiveness. Practicing assertiveness means you are not at the mercy of the big, bad world around you; you are capable of meeting your own needs. When he witnesses you confidently voicing your salad preference, he is going to feel the weight of a thousand anchovies lifted off his shoulders: "Phew, this one's not going to expect me to make her night for her. Clearly she's able to go ahead and take care of herself. Good thing, because I'm so bowled over by her Southwest Georgia O'Keeffe–like outfit that I can barely concentrate on the menu . . ."

A SPECIFIC VICINITY

It is not necessary to identify *exactly* what you're hankering for every single moment for this technique to be effective. As moods and circumstances shift, you should naturally adapt to the changing winds. Being open to suggestion and compromise is essential to all interaction. So if a decision needs to be made and you are unsure of the specifics of your desires, just provide some solid adjectives to get the ball rolling.

For example, your date has taken you to see his roommate's fledgling jazz band's first gig. After the show, not wanting to end the evening, your guy suggests getting a bite to eat. Like a gentleman, he asks what type of cuisine you are craving. You may not have a specific yearning for any particular food, but instead of replying with one of those drab mutterings of indifference, set the night in motion with a series of descriptive phrases. Such as

"Well, I'd love to be in a place that's cozy and candlelit, but still lively with energy—possibly outside. I see rock salt in wooden bowls, and maybe saffron or turmeric in most of the dishes. Warm food, a comforting menu, nothing too cold or crunchy . . . Yes, something like that would be nice."

It's unlikely that the exact scene you've just described will actually materialize, but that's not the purpose of this play. Proposing an ambience and offering your ideal sensual experience moves the evening forward. Instead of standing on a street corner awkwardly flip-flopping between heading east or west in hopes of happening upon a suitable spot, you've given the mission direction. Your clarity of purpose will spark the synapses in his brain, allowing him to remember that cute little joint where his taste buds last touched turmeric. And while you are savoring your samosas, he'll be watching your satisfied smile and eagerly awaiting the inspired adjectives you will use to describe the perfect dessert. "Warm, gushy, spongy, lactose-free . . ."

And why would he bother to make such an effort? Well, only for the simple fact that men *love* to please. Inside, your man desires nothing more than to play Stanley to your Stella and give you the kind of pleasure you'd never dare abandon. They yearn to deliver fulfillment and excitement, and watch your cheeks glow pink with delight. They want to be the guy who really *does it* for you, but sadly, they don't always know how. It's not uncommon for many a great man to sorely miss the mark.

This failure to satisfy can be devastating to the sensitive male ego, but we can't blame them for misinterpreting our elusive, ephemeral signs—if you can even call them signs. Leaving your Langston Hughes collection out on the countertop does not guarantee there'll be a ticket to the banks of the Mississippi River under the tree come Christmas. Men don't get the difference between soy-based and synthetic, or tulle and taffeta. They're not that subtle. This is why you must tell them! It's not a pain in the ass to try to fulfill your rock-salted, candlelit vision; it's a relief! They have a starting point, a clear and definite aim, a certified ticket to your gratification. They're not left ambling in the dark trying to interpret what "whatever" really means. Your indecisiveness makes them insecure. And rightly so; it's impossible to please a lady who won't give an inkling of insight into what she wants. And stirring deep insecurity in your guy on the first date is not the most ideal move. So save the symbolism for the stage, and for goodness's sake, just pick a place to eat!

PLAYING THE ANGEL

Our final point in defense of decisiveness is that it will at the very least set the stage for you to be respected. The man who pines for an opinionless lady is the man whose primary goal is to dominate— not a good starting point for an equal and loving partnership. By making it clear that you not only have opinions, but also at times *act on* them, you quickly weed out any riffraff that might harbor antiquated ideas about "the weaker sex." If he can't handle your empowered ability to state that you'd like to go to a hamburger joint instead of a steak house, pretty soon he's going to try to ride herd on all your personal decisions. Better cut your losses and get outta Dodge before he brings you back to his Airstream and tries to make you scrub his floors, soak his socks, or shine his shamrock.

So next time you find yourself on a streetcar of desire, don't just ride it wherever it happens to take you and hop off at any old stop. Get clear on where you'd really like to go. Then declare to your dreamy driver the exact destination that will ring your bell, and take note of his gaze of adoration as he puts the pedal to the metal and speeds the two of you off in just the right direction.

SMUTTY MOUTH

*While sharing a smoke, you allow some smut
to spill from those ladylike lips*

Propriety certainly has its place when playing for love, but we know you ain't no saint. In the midst of your well-mannered ways, permitting your streak of naughtiness to bust through will give your man copious material for his next confessional. His impure ponderings are a sure sign of your undeniable allure. So go ahead, unchain those unseemly thoughts and give your old Catholic school nuns reason to pray for your sullied soul.

Masterful flirtation, as you know, requires the full allowance of your real impulses. Yet the rules of social etiquette can sometimes restrict the full expression of our authenticity. We are taught to be polite, smile, put our napkin on our lap, never uncross our legs, never leave the house without a bra, and never say what we are really thinking, for fear we'll be branded as surly little sluts. Look, we totally advocate for good manners. We know the value of sending thank-you notes and chewing with our mouth closed. But sometimes all the dedication to decorum can be a real drag. Sometimes we need to let our natural naughty side out to stretch her legs, kick up her slip, and cause a little stir.

Broaching a seriously taboo subject or slipping in a choice four-letter word might be exactly what your inner devil wants and what the conversation needs. Pushing the envelope in social interaction is ballsy and exciting. It's insanely sexy to see a woman who clearly knows all the rules of social politesse *still choose* to tell that joke about the lonesome farmer and his herd of sheep just as her braised sausage and fennel entrée arrives at the table.

SMUTTING STYLES

Each of us has a different level of comfort with our naughty side. Some women could sit through a twelve-hour porn marathon without batting an eye; some blush when they even hear the word "prick." But you don't have to be into bestiality to practice this technique. You can simply tailor it to your comfort level and natural urges. So if you are the type of woman who is truly stimulated by the twisted things in life, go ahead and retell the story you read about the poor middle-aged man whose cock-binding venture went painfully wrong. Or if you just enjoy the simple thrill of declaring your militant boss a flaming bitch, let it rip. Both approaches will have him squirming in his seat—for very different reasons, of course, but either way, your bit of bad-girl demeanor will guarantee that the evening never gets caught in the death trap of tedious niceness. We'd rather be surly little sluts any day.

However, instead of spending the whole evening using your sizable cache of colorful language to discuss the trials and tribulations of your last colonoscopy, optimally you should just touch upon this technique and then move on. This way you will reveal a slip of contradiction, a trace of paradox, a sprig of poison ivy in your otherwise innocent herb garden—without killing the encounter with an infestation of foulness.

Our friend Aviva recently toyed with this technique and delivered an impressive account of its effect:

Aviva is a bright, bubbly young lady who happens to have a rather dark sense of humor. Though she is generally courteous and mannerly, she has always maintained a real appreciation for the inappropriate. While browsing the aisles of a New Age bookstore one Saturday afternoon, Aviva struck up a conversation with a cute guy who kept cropping up in her same section. After some initial banter, he asked if she would like to join him at the café for a hot cup of something. While sipping vanilla chais, they compared notes on all the spiritual, psycho-scientific books they had each read, discussing astral projection, properties of the root chakra, the Mayan calendar, and the like. "I mean, it was all really interesting stuff. I read those sorts of books and I like to discuss those subjects and everything, but it was getting kind of lofty and existential. This guy was so cute; I just knew he was more playful than he was letting on. So I was sitting there listening to him talk about some Ayurvedic philosophy on kidney stones, and I blurted out, 'What would you rather do, fuck your fourth-grade teacher, or bite into a cube of zits?' Man, was he surprised! I think he was expecting me to ask whether he'd rather meet Buddha or Einstein or something! He was blushing so hard and kept laughing so much, he could barely answer the question! Finally, he said he'd rather bite into a cube of zits, because he was pretty sure his fourth-grade teacher was dead. Things were a hell of a lot more entertaining after that. When he asked me for my number, he said he'd never met a girl who could talk about metaphysics and invoke images of sex with a septuagenarian in the same conversation before." Sweet, right?

A TIME AND PLACE

Adapting your smut to your environment is crucial. You won't win any hearts by cursing like a drunken sailor just as the lights go down in the theater because you've already lost your "goddamned, stupid Playbill." Being rude in public or impinging on others' space is bad, unsexy form. If you are in a rowdy, crowded, honky-tonk bar, you've got more leeway than in an intimate, candlelit eatery with communal tables. And bellowing a few profanities at a hockey player will fly much better than flipping the bird at a golf pro.

Consider your geographical location as well. For example, our friend Michele has reported that New York men are a lot less shocked by smutty tongues than the corn-fed fellows down in Nashville, where she grew up. "Even a pinch of profanity can send those southern boys for a loop!" she warns. We are not saying deny your true self in order to accommodate a man's standard, but being aware of what you are working with is always smart. It's no fun to offend if it's severely offensive. After all, we are intelligent, considerate, thoughtful ladies, and being sensitive to our dates' customs is plain old decent human behavior.

Furthermore, as we have mentioned many times before, cruelty toward others is something we do not endorse. We are well aware that certain people are infuriating nitwits, but unleashing an artillery of violently crude vilifications will only make you look like an angry meany. However, a creative comparison between the vulturelike local politician preying on innocent interns and the scary Skeksis from *The Dark Crystal* could be amusingly appropriate. Or noting the similarities between your creepy lavender lotion–lathering yoga teacher and David Koresh would probably be more comical than callous. Just be sure to remain gracious and compassionate, even if the woman sitting next to you is dosed with so many petroleum-based synthetics, she reeks like a five-dollar hooker, or the man in front of you has a scalp that's so scabby, it looks like a bargain-basement circumcision. Better to remember the universal motivator ("We all just want love!") and keep those thoughts tucked safely away.

SHERPA FLASH

With this immodest technique, you can run the risk of overstimulation. Some-times hearing just the slightest smudge of smut will cause a man to believe you're the kind of girl who's up for everything and anything. As a result, he may plow through your boundaries, putting your personal safety at risk. To avoid this potentially icky situation, it's important to modulate your technique. Let slip just a little smut here and there and get out fast. Drop your dirty grenade and then quickly turn in another less provocative direction as though it never happened. So by the time he realizes what he heard, you've already moved on to discussing the antique coin collection your great-aunt so kindly be-queathed to you in her will. And if he strikes you as the type that will jump at any excuse to get inappropriately kinky or nasty, it's probably best to avoid this technique altogether (actually, you should probably avoid *him* altogether). Practice your smut with a bit of discretion so you can uphold your boundaries while also stilling his pounding heart.

CONFESSIONS OF A DIRTY DAME

When experimenting with the flirtatious potential of your lewd and lascivious conduct, one of the surest inroads to take is the path of self-deprecation. By being comfortable with making yourself the butt of a joke, you demonstrate inner confidence and present a refreshingly unexpected front for an otherwise lovely young lady.

The following from our friend Courtney is an exceptional example of the power of self-deprecating smut:

Courtney is a classically beautiful, somewhat stately young woman. She certainly has a wild side, but it's usually not the first thing she shows when meeting new people. One evening, while at the opening reception for a young art collectors' club, she was sipping free wine and examining one of the pieces—a semi-abstract painting of a figure hunched over with his arms folded across his body, his head thrown back and mouth open. As she pondered the piece, an older man, maybe early forties, definitely attractive, made his way over. You know the gallery scene: gorgeous girl standing alone, drinking wine, a perfect first-liner made readily available by the artwork on the wall. Anyway, he picked up his cue and started commenting on the intense agony and pain of the figure, how the artist really expressed the deep sorrow and mourning in the body language, and so on. Finally, he turned to Courtney and asked if she agreed, to which she said, "Well, I see your point, but no, I had a totally different take on it. It actually reminds me of this time I shat in my pants. He looks just like I did when it happened. I was laughing so hard, I couldn't control myself! It might also have something to do with the gloppy oil paint in the corner over there." Yes, a kind of grossly inappropriate thing to say. But it was the truth, so why lie? It was what she was thinking. And she had been really happy when she shat her pants. She was ecstatic with laughter.

"Anyway," Courtney recalls, "he was old enough to be over that girls-don't-poop bullshit; I knew he could handle it. And even though it's a pretty unflattering, highly embarrassing story to tell about oneself, he was obviously delighted—he followed me around the whole night!" Later that week he took her to dinner, and after the meal he jokingly suggested she skip the coffee and have a glass of port instead.

Though Courtney's divulgence might at first make her seem filthy and repulsive (shitting your pants is not the most elegant of acts), the story had the opposite effect. Her free-spirited attitude, especially when it came to her own hilarious mishap, made her all the more enticing. She doesn't mind being seen as an occasional pants-crapper because she knows she's the bomb no matter what's oozing out of her anus at any given moment. Her ability to reveal that unflattering aspect of herself showed *extreme confidence,* which is the ultimate and most definitive measure of sexiness. No amount of soil in her capris could ever weigh down such a bodalicious babe.

There is another, more obscure dynamic that plays an important role in this example. Men behave in weird and disgusting ways. They have strange habits; letting farts slip at inopportune moments, missing the toilet bowl in the early morning, and displaying a general childlike cluelessness that seems to permeate many of their actions. Yet they yearn deeply, probably even more so than women, for unconditional love and acceptance. To see a woman like Courtney have enough perspective, humor, and lightheartedness to not only laugh at her own messy past, but also share it without hesitation or embarrassment is like an answer to their secret prayers. By displaying such an unprecedented amount of self-acceptance, the man feels that she just might understand, tolerate, and even love him for all of his own dirty faults—and *nothing* feels better than that. It is such an exquisitely rare quality that unless the guy is so out of touch he can't recognize the gem standing before him, he'll go to any length to secure her presence in his ketchup-stained, toe-fungused, ball-scratching world.

The foulness that flows from your ladylike lips is a fiendishly exciting aspect of your authenticity. So during the first encounter, don't hesitate to let all your wicked witticisms and profane ponderances climb up from the depths of their dank dwelling and spend a little time in the sun. You'll be surprised at how adept those little devils are at capturing your man's soul. So give them a chance to do their worst—they just might engorge his heart to the size of . . . well, you get the point. Need we say more?

A SECOND OF SILENCE

*Despite the chitter and chatter of a Friday night crowd,
you hold his gaze for an unabashed second of silence*

Shhh . . . the sound of silence is an aphrodisiac that is all too often overlooked. A single moment of quiet recognition between you and your man might be all that is needed to ensure his complete captivation. So during the first encounter or date, take a moment to give your vocal cords a rest, look him in the eye, and let the power of silence electrify him with unspoken magic.

Continuous chatter is common when meeting someone new. Dialogue is often used to calm the nerves and avoid awkward silences. But this final technique encourages you to resist the urge toward static noise. Let the conversation drop for a second and simply look into his eyes for an extra beat. By doing this, you make space for a flash of acknowledgement that goes deep beneath the surface babble and instantly triggers a subatomic connection.

So when he's finished verbalizing his thoughts on the monumental effect the incandescent filament lightbulb had on the lives of late-nineteenth-century Americans, instead of immediately nodding in agreement and sharing your two cents, pause, look him in the eye, and don't speak a word. Simply hold his gaze. Give it just one bold extra moment where you don't rush in, but don't withdraw, either. Silent eye contact is wildly magnetic; it cuts straight to the core with lightning speed—charging your communication with a level of stimulation that's just not possible to *talk* your way into.

WORDS ARE VERY UNNECESSARY

This technique is possibly the boldest of the eight (depending on the severity of your smuttiness). A few seconds of quietude gives both of you the chance to be fully present in each other's company in a uniquely intimate way. With words pushed aside, a purer part of your essence has room to emerge. As you hold his gaze for that extra soundless beat, you begin to bare your true self. Stripped of the stories, opinions, and theories that protect and distract, in that simple space of wordless connection you become naked—vulnerable, open, and real.

Which is obviously what makes this technique so effective, and so freaking nerve-wracking to employ! It can feel scary to be so open. The thought of such intimacy, even just for a few seconds, can really frazzle the nerves. But the self-realizing woman is safe in her vulnerability. She can risk being exposed because she's not afraid of what might be found. Inviting a moment of silence conveys absolute confidence. The woman who's got the gall to strip away her cover-up of pronouns, verbs, and adjectives and be completely at ease in her virtual nakedness is sure to jam the circuits of any worthy heartthrob.

For example, say one day you are attending a lecture on the birth of electromagnetics, learning how certain scientific contributions in that arena sparked the Second Industrial Revolution in the late 1880s. During the coffee break, you and a dapper young man in well-worn corduroys and horn-rimmed glasses find yourselves reaching for the same paper cup. So you naturally fall into a conversation about the genius of Nikola Tesla and his unconventional experimentations. "You know, I hadn't realized he invented the radio," you remark while stirring in some half-and-half. "Oh yes," the bespectacled man in corduroy offers, "he pioneered the whole field of wireless communication . . ."

As he continues to explain alternating current electric power, you begin to notice how cute his lips are when he forms his syllables, and how sweet it was for him to pour your scalding-hot coffee to ensure that you wouldn't get burned. Yes, it's true; you are starting to like him. So as his sentences come to a close, as opposed to jumping in and adding to the subject, you don't say anything. You don't even nod; you just look him in the eye for a long moment, possibly adding a hint of a smile, and eventually turn back to your creamer. At this point be sure to grab some napkins because he will most certainly spill his beverage in nervous anticipation as he takes a seat at your side for the remainder of the lecture. But that's the kind of stunning effect you must expect from this particular brand of wireless communication.

SHERPA FLASH

In this age of handheld technology, it can be tempting to manage your first encounter/date nerves by keeping your mobile device close at hand and sinking your attention into it whenever there's a lull. But as a self-realizing woman, you don't need that cold, hard, little safety blanket to survive the evening. Make a point of turning it off when there's a man in your midst that's worth a chance. Put your little friend away so you can give him your full attention, and expect that he will do the same. This tiny gesture of consideration for the full-blooded human before you will send a powerful message. It will show that your sense of security is not gained from the number of messages you receive in a day. You are able to be present and engage fully. So cut the cord with your handheld and wire your encounter with genuine kindness and respect.

SILENT REVERIE

In our current culture, silence has been pushed so far onto the back burner, it has basically fallen behind the stove to smolder and rot with the dirty dust bunnies and dead roaches. There it lies, choking, sputtering, desperately needing resuscitation. But what can it do? It can't call for help. It's silence! So you'll have to seek it out on your own, without a flashy commercial or pop-up ad to remind you. The noisiest messages out there tend to get all the attention—screaming about what you should be doing, buying, listening to, and talking about. Silence isn't such a hot topic because there's no way to package and sell it. In fact, just by talking about it, you have already spoiled it. Nice job.

But did you ever lie on your back in a dewy field beneath a star-strewn sky with only the faint sound of the wind rustling in far-off trees and a couple of crickets chirping in the tall grass? Have you ever gotten lost in the autumn woods and instead of panicking and searching for help, sat down on a soft bed of moss and just surrendered to the vastness of nature? Or have you ever paddled a canoe so far out into a lake that you could no longer hear the sounds from shore, only the soft lapping of water against your boat?

All the great mystics, from Rumi to Rilke to Rabia, know that ultimate peace and freedom exist only when we shatter the fortress of ideas we've built around ourselves and open our minds to a world without definition. Only then can we transcend the limitations of form. Fortunately, you don't need to cut out your own tongue to get in touch with your Buddha nature. You can start gently by taking a Thoreau-style sojourn all by your lonesome out into the natural world.

So switch off your cell phone, wrap up your headphones, get yourself offline, and stride out the door with absolutely nothing to distract you from the divinity of the unspoken. You needn't make it all the way to Walden Pond, but do try to get farther than your front walk before racing back to check your e-mail. Find a gentle brook, statuesque boulder, or deserted street bench where you will not be distracted by the noise of the modern world. And when you get there, do absolutely nothing. Attempt to not even think. Just sit back and enjoy as the silence floods your inner ears.

You might at first feel an icky rush of panic. *I should check my voice mail. Oh, I forgot to pick up the dry cleaning. Are the beans in the fridge rotten? Maybe I should grab some on the way home. This feels strange. Those authors are weirdos. They'd better be right about this making me a better flirt. I feel alone. I feel unanchored. I really want to call my mom.* But resist the urge to run away from yourself! Stay with silence and you will eventually break through the anxiety and arrive at a place of comfort in your solitude and stillness.

Being at ease in this realm will take practice, but it is a most worthy tool to have tucked in your pocket. It will keep you from feeling unbearably awkward if you're sitting alone in a bar waiting for a tardy friend, or overly self-conscious when walking into a party solo, or so needy for companionship that you bring home whatever lonesome soul happens to be nearest the door as you make your exit. Comfort with your quiet solitude provides you with inner self-reliance, which translates directly to inner confidence—the key to brilliant flirtation. Although he was accused of lacking ambition, we are certain that Thoreau knew exactly what he was doing alone out there in the woods. *Oh, Henry, you old dog, we had no idea you were so practiced in the art of coquetry! It would have been quite a treat to be the shop girl providing your weekly provisions.*

SHEDDING THE ACT

Usually we keep our secrets concealed, never revealing that we actually like the gentleman before us, or want to pursue more of a relationship. Out of embarrassment or fear that the interest is not mutual, we veil our desire behind conversation and avoid eye contact with shy, girlish giggles and furtive glances.

But a moment of silent eye contact taps into the subtext of the situation like nothing else can. It's like talking without speaking. Holding his gaze for that extra second says, "The jig is up! I like you. We both know why we're here, so let's not beat around the bush." It is the bold action of a grown-up woman who is confident enough in herself and her appeal to momentarily make her desires known.

We understand that this is not always an easy move. We've been taught that a lady should be demure and unassuming, never forward in the pursuit of her wants, never admitting that she craves intimacy, pleasure, or companionship. So when a handsome man looks in our direction from across the room, we instantly turn away, hiding our eyes in order to not expose our interest or let him think we might possibly have been looking his way too. Talk about a lost signal!

But this technique tells you to take a risk by looking right back at him—allowing yourself to see and be seen. For just a few seconds, let your attraction be apparent instead of pretending it doesn't exist. Through that shared eye contact, a current of energy will be generated between the two of you. Whether he's across the dance floor or across the table, your silent look will give him a window of opportunity. It will let him know you are turned on by his attentions, which will translate to an instant boost of encouragement (and men need boosts of encouragement!). After a moment like that, he'll have no choice but to saunter over and ask for a dance, lean over and ask for a date, or slide over and ask if he could pretty-please join you for a drink.

Observe how our friend Christyn implemented this tantalizing technique one summer evening in Vermont:

Christyn is the quintessential earth woman. From the soles of her well-worn Birkenstocks to the tip of her long blond braid to her sun sign in Taurus, she thoroughly embodies the warmth and abundance of Mother Earth. Her love of the natural world has taken her hiking and camping for weeks at a time deep in the forest with little more than a one-hitter and a tattered copy of *Silent Spring* on hand. But like many other earthlings, she knew that her love of nature wasn't going to keep her warm at night the way a hot-blooded woodsman could. So she couldn't help but take note when a blue-eyed, heavily bearded, warmhearted wild

SHERPA FLASH

It is essential that you recognize the power of this play. Chatter creates a buffer zone where two beings can keep their distance. So dropping the noise and just letting the pure connection happen is going to instantly ramp up the heat. When perched across the way from a gentleman, if you choose to hold his gaze for that extra silent beat, he's *going* to notice. You are sending a crystal clear message. So if there's no room in your lean-to for the particular man in your sights, please—do not employ this technique. This one should only be used when you actually like the guy, when you want more of his time and attention. Just as you would not tempt a wild bear cub, you should not toy with a silent stare. You could end up in some very hot water, and we're not talking about the bubbly sulfuric spring you stumbled upon during your last mountain trek.

man showed up as a fellow counselor at the environmental ed camp where she was working.

One chilly night as they sat around the campfire singing songs with the kids, Christyn's heart brimmed as she witnessed the bearded woodsman's enthusiastic participation in the music. Suddenly, mid-song, his eyes flicked up and met hers. "Now, I would normally have looked away, not wanting him to know I was watching him or liked him or anything, but this time I held my gaze. It made me nervous, but the truth is I *did* like him! What was so wrong with showing it? The vibe between us was so strong, I knew he had to feel it." Later that evening the woodsman took his chance and moved a bit closer to earth mama's end of the log, and from then on, goose down wasn't the only thing keeping Christyn toasty at night.

SILENT TREATMENT

It is entirely possible to short-circuit a perfectly fine flirtatious encounter by overdoing this technique. Remember, the idea is to give a little flash of connected silence, a moment where the two of you are looking at one another without distraction or noise. This is not about creepily holding his gaze until your eyeballs start to dry up. If in doubt, make the second of silence so brief, it might never have happened, leaving him guessing as to whether he was imagining the entire affair.

Furthermore, do not execute your second of silence with a frown on your face or a furrow in your brow. The point is not to make him feel like he's got mustard on his chin or a crazy nose hair twisting around his nostril. Neither is it a blank stare, as if you don't know what on Earth he's talking about, or worse, don't care. These kinds of mixed messages could really fry his switchboard and blow the whole experiment. Your second of silence should be a warm, engaged, present, alive, quiet few moments when you make the conscious choice to allow the beating of your hearts to be the only sound.

So as you're sitting there sipping your Lemon Zinger and he finishes his monologue on the catastrophe of his adolescent bar mitzvah speech, make like a Carthusian monk and dare not speak a word. Look him in the eye, strip down to your bare essence, and give your spirits the chance to fuse. The connection will really start to crackle when you allow yourself to simply enjoy the silence.

CONCLUSION

—◦⟨3⟩◦—

Flirting, as a concept, doesn't always get the credit it deserves. At the outset of this journey, you may have assumed that flirting was only for the empty-headed, but now you know it's actually for the curious-minded. You may have thought flirting was just a sugary puff of whipped air that dissolves the moment it touches the tongue, but now you see that it packs the full nutritious punch of a well-balanced meal. You may have believed that flirting was something you do for men, but upon walking the path toward flirtatious mastery, you now understand that flirting is something you do for yourself.

As you go forth and begin to enact these new techniques and concepts, know that your experiences will not always be ideal. There will undoubtedly be a lot of balls flying in your direction, and you might get smacked in the ear with the unexpected. Sometimes when expressing your intelligence, you'll find yourself tongue-tied and mumbling. Or in a moment of enthusiastic arm gesticulation, you might knock over the water cooler. Or maybe after you reveal a particularly strange and exciting secret thought, he'll look totally baffled, resulting in a profound moment of complete awkwardness. That's okay. The point is not perfection. Flirting is a play between two people, a back-and-forth volley, and sometimes someone might drop the ball. But with practice you will learn to just roll with it and enjoy the game even when it doesn't seem to be going your way. You'll trust that your realness is still the best thing you've got going.

Something else you might notice when practicing your flirting skills is that men will react very differently to your radiance, depending on their particular personality. They may respond with kindness, excitement, curiosity, intimidation, sarcasm, or even subtle hostility. It's up to you to be honest about your intuition and discerning about what you choose to share with whom. As you volley, you will need to make decisions in the moment about how much to reveal to him. Sometimes you'll feel perfectly safe and able to play freely. Other times you will feel he's returning the balls a bit too forcefully and might be more interested in winning than creating a healthy connection. In those moments, remember that you always have the option to call it a day and walk off the court. There is no reason to engage with a man who does not have your best interests and comfort at heart. Never lie about your gut feeling. It's better not to play than to be involved in an exchange that puts your well-being at risk.

Another important point is that even though you may be at the top of your game, the man may simply not want to play. We all experience rejection in this life. All of us have had the experience of wanting someone who doesn't seem to return our interest. This is natural, and should be expected at times. So instead of taking it personally and plummeting into self-hatred and self-doubt, remember that you have no idea what is making him turn away. He might be involved in a relationship, recently heartbroken, intimidated by your awesomeness, or you might remind him of his baby sister, and the thought of intimacy with you gives him the heebie-jeebies. There are so many possibilities that it would be silly and irrational to jump to the conclusion that his rejection is the result of some sort of deficiency on your part. In these moments, we suggest that you allow yourself to fully feel any disappointment that arises, and then fully let it go. Move on and find another court to play in. You do not want to be with a man who does not want to be with you. This would be an imbalanced, unpleasant mismatch. Sometimes your instincts recognize the mismatch; sometimes the guy's instincts spot it first. Either way, this information needs to be respected. It will never do you any good to lie about what's in the air and continue pursuing a man who's incapable of providing the affection you seek.

The choice to *not lie* is profoundly liberating. The eight flirtation techniques are about upholding your personal integrity; they are essentially about *not lying.* By expressing your enthusiasm, allowing your femininity to flourish, or letting slip a touch of twisted humor, you are making a statement. You are saying, "This is really what's happening, right now, and I will not lie about it. I will not quell my excitement for this hibiscus hand lotion, I will not repress my urge to drape myself with white gossamer lace, and I will not ignore the obvious fact that my muddled tomato drink closely resembles an early-stage miscarriage." Brilliant flirtation is so empowering because it depends upon your living and functioning truthfully. By making the decision to not lie to yourself or to others, you are able to stand firmly and unapologetically on your own two feet. You have nothing to hide. You are completely engaged with life. And by being engaged with life, you will become totally engaging, and will therefore naturally engage just the right man as well.

The steps you have taken to become a self-realizing woman and the techniques you have learned for brilliant flirtation will, unquestionably, help you find your best possible partner. Throughout this journey, you have been cultivating your sincerity and integrity. You have been deepening the quality of the

relationship you have with yourself. By upholding your commitment to your personal values, you will recognize men who are
operating at a similar level of self-respect and personal dignity.
You will easily identify the types that would only perpetuate your
past pain and suffering, and will instead be drawn to those who
will support and advance the emergence of your unique spirit.
Which is exactly what we hope for you!

Brilliant flirtation has come to embody our philosophy on
how to live, and we hope it brings you just as much joy and satisfaction as it has us. We know that you are beautiful on the inside
and the outside. We know that you contain a perfectly unique
jewel of truth that is flawless and priceless. We wish with all our
hearts that you will spend the rest of your life basking in love—
from friends, family, super-sexy men, and most importantly, from
within. With one final request we bid you adieu. The next time
you reclaim your kingdom from your inner damsel in distress,
create an outfit based solely on the iridescent tones of the feather
you found on your last twilight stroll, or mesmerize a man with
your knowledge of iron-forging methods in sixteenth-century
Europe, please think of your dear old sherpas and how we helped
you realize how exceptional, lovable, irresistible . . . how very
*Smitten*esque you truly are.